Mr Gibson
ticket machine

This book is dedicated to the memory of George Sawyer

First published 2021

ISBN 978 1 85414 465 2

Published by Capital Transport Publishing Ltd
www.capitaltransport.com

Printed in the EU

Mr Gibson's ticket machine

The complete story
1944-1993

Anthony Cross

Capital Transport

Contents

Cover: The man and his creation; George Gibson pictured with the machine that bears his name.

Opposite Title Page: A production Gibson in use. This famous publicity shot, by Colin Tait, dates from February 1955 when the machine illustrated, No 5886, was new. Remarkably, this machine still survives in a private collection.
© *TfL from the London Transport Museum collection*

Acknowledgements

Without input from a lot of key people, this publication, like the Gibson ticket machine itself, would never have materialised.

We have George Gibson to thank for conceiving the machine in those dark days of the Second World War and as Superintendent of London Transport's Stockwell Punch Works, the man responsible for building the first ones and for giving it its name. But there are a host of others too, who would otherwise be unrecognised for their part in the story.

Among these men is Charles Speller, Gibson's successor, who was responsible for shaping the machine that would eventually go into production and who may well have built the early prototypes. We should also recognise too the part played by B.H.F. Benford, London Transport's Fares and Charges Officer for his faith in the prototype machine and David McKenna, their Commercial Manager who skilfully navigated the obstacles getting it built in volume. David Colville is another otherwise unknown personality that loomed large in the early days, McKenna's opposite number at Crawley Ticket Machines, the firm that won the contract to build the Gibson machine. So too J.L. Flynn of R.M.R. Engineering who headed the production team at Tring.

And of course no history of the Gibson ticket machine would be complete without the name of George Sawyer, to whom this book is dedicated. As a young man, George helped build some of the first production machines and later as the last Superintendent of London Transport's Effra Road Ticket Machine Works, presided over the metamorphosis of the Gibson to overcome the challenges of decimalisation and fares inflation in the 1970s. He also directed the search for a replacement but perhaps his greatest achievement was keeping the marque alive for so long. More than double its planned service life of 20 years in response to the unique set of challenges posed by a dramatic turnaround in policy when London Transport decided, contrary to expectation, not to end conductors and Routemaster buses in the 1980s.

Above all though George was a gentleman who always welcomed enthusiasts with kindness and generosity until his untimely death. He left a legacy of otherwise unknown records and artefacts kindly made available by his daughter Julie, without whose help this publication would not have been possible.

Very special thanks too should be given to the London Transport Museum Depot at Acton for the generous use of their extensive photographic library, which contains unique official views showing Gibson machines in use in a variety of hands and settings. Without these photographs, this publication would lack the human dimension that the subject so richly deserves.

My grateful thanks also for the kind and conscientious co-operation and support from staff members at both Acton and the Transport for London Corporate Archives, who facilitated access to over 6000 documents held in storage that span the entire period covered by this book. The task of calling these up, sifting through them and painstakingly photographing each one fell on Damon Cross. Similarly without his help and generosity in sharing this material, supplemented by his collection of photographic and ticket evidence, pen and paper on the subject would never have met.

Particular thanks too to Andrew Jeffreys for sharing his early drafts on the mechanisation of London's ticketing system and providing copious encouragement and advice and proof reading the finished manuscript. Likewise my sincere gratitude for Laurie Akehurst's input who proved extremely knowledgable about all aspects of London's bus operations and in particular the minefield of fare revisions. Bob Wingrove and David Harman too have both proved to be a fount of knowledge on bus ticketing and I must acknowledge at this juncture the methodical and scholarly publications and presentations of the Transport Ticket Society which have yielded much useful data.

Uncredited photographs are from my own collection or of machines I have received for repair and servicing at various times and I acknowledge my gratitude to the owners for allowing me to photograph them.

Finally I must mention Peter Brooks who authored the short but authoritative treatise on the Gibson machine in an article published in the London Bus Magazine as long ago as 1988. This has for long been the recognised authority on the subject and only now, with more extensive access to archive material, can the complete story be told of "Mr Gibson's ticket machine".

Anthony Cross, June 2021

Introduction

The year 2021 marked 75 years since the first Gibson A14 ticket machine entered trial service with London Transport. But while the capital's integrated public transport undertaking might have been expected to be at the forefront of innovation, in reality it came to the table rather late in the day in devising a mechanical means of issuing tickets on its road transport operations. This was in contrast to the rail division, which was mechanised and partially automated far sooner.

It would be unfair to suggest this was due to the conservatism for its own sake of the London Passenger Transport Board's senior management. In vehicle design and engineering generally, London Transport was in many respects the industry leader. While it is true to say that the laborious punch system for validating travel was both slow and expensive, and wholly at odds with a progressive and modern transport authority, its principal advantage lay in that it worked.

In the years leading up to the Second World War, none of the proprietary ticket machine designs were sufficiently effective or robust to persuade the Board to abandon its punch tickets, although various trials and experiments were conducted as new products appeared on the market.

George Gibson would have had the job of keeping the relatively few ticket machines in his care in serviceable condition, all inherited from constituent concerns on the formation of London Transport in 1933. It would have been apparent to him that commercially produced equipment was constructed to lower standards and used inferior materials than the operating conditions in London demanded. To better the most appropriate commercial machine available at that time, the TIM (an acronym of 'ticket issuing machine'), which could account for up to nine different fare values, any new design would not only need to have superior build quality but the capability of issuing tickets of ten or more such values.

Gibson would have well understood the often elaborate mechanical principles needed to produce a machine capable of printing all the necessary journey variables on a blank roll of paper. In addition, absolute reliability in accounting for all money taken was critical. Failure in that department would have undermined both the confidence of road staff as well as the important task of revenue generation. Fortunately the Gibson machine performed its allotted task admirably.

This is a story of the conception and birth of the Gibson machine and the reasons for the long gestation between the appearance of workable prototypes in trial use in August 1945 (albeit with ten fare values) and the first production machines of 1953. Delays were encountered over patenting the invention and production in the early years was plagued by materials shortages in the bleak post-war austerity era, not helped by numerous changes to the specification in the light of operational exigency and experience.

Of the 17,000 production machines built, an estimated 10% or so survive with private individuals and a small number still earn their keep for various firms providing a 'London bus' experience. Until very recently, they could still be found in revenue use on the Epping-Ongar Railway heritage route 339.

While the Gibson predates the AEC/PRV Routemaster by a decade, the two are often associated. In reality Gibson ticket machines graced the full range of crew operated London Transport buses and trolleybuses from the 1950s to the 1990s.

This book is intended for the tens of thousands of staff that used them as part of their working lives, as well as the countless modern devotees who somehow find the mechanism a source of delight and interest.

Gibson Anatomy

Some basic understanding of how the machine is put together will help where there are references later to particular major components.

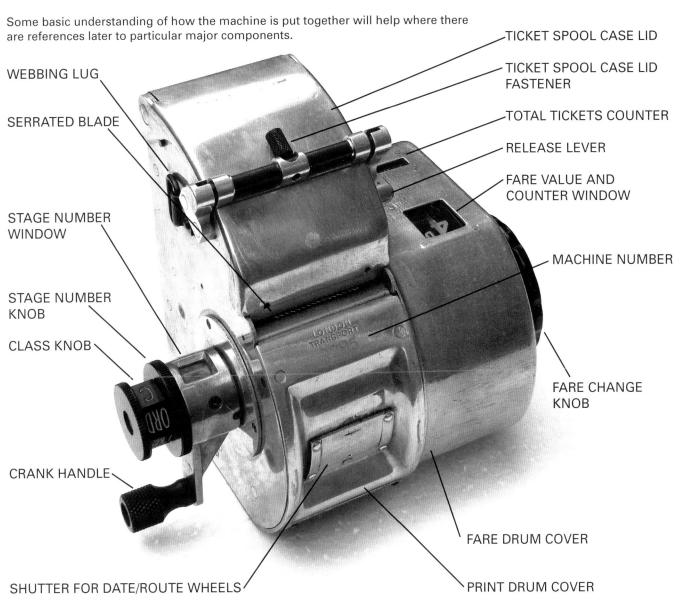

WEBBING LUG

SERRATED BLADE

STAGE NUMBER WINDOW

STAGE NUMBER KNOB

CLASS KNOB

CRANK HANDLE

SHUTTER FOR DATE/ROUTE WHEELS

TICKET SPOOL CASE LID

TICKET SPOOL CASE LID FASTENER

TOTAL TICKETS COUNTER

RELEASE LEVER

FARE VALUE AND COUNTER WINDOW

MACHINE NUMBER

FARE CHANGE KNOB

FARE DRUM COVER

PRINT DRUM COVER

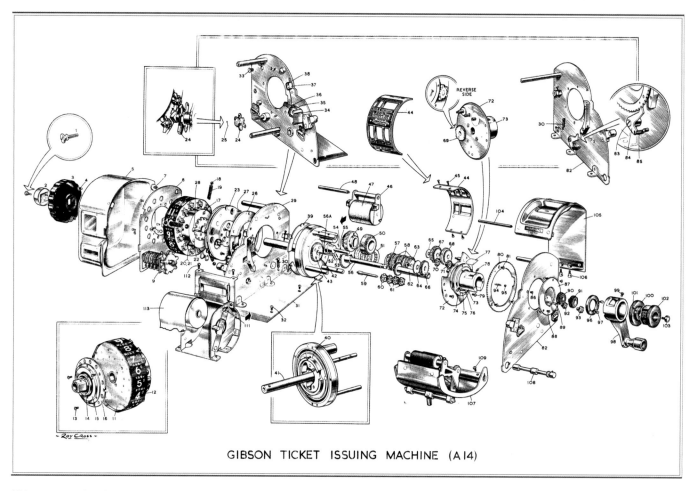

GIBSON TICKET ISSUING MACHINE (A14)

This cutaway drawing was commissioned by London Transport in the late 1950s/early 1960s to assist in maintenance and servicing. By a strange coincidence, the illustrator, Roy Cross, is my father and also undertook similar drawings for the RT bodies built by Saunders–Roe and famously, for the AEC/PRV Routemaster. I was only aware of his involvement with the Gibson by accident when rummaging through a box of Gibson parts that had originated from the Isle of Man where the machines were once used. Rolled up in a tube was this drawing and my eye was immediately drawn to the signature.

It would have been necessary for my father to visit Effra Road where the various components would have been set out on a bench in the sequence shown and photographed by him. The drawing would then have been produced from these photographs with the parts themselves to hand as reference. Overall the machine contains 689 parts, mostly arranged in various sub-assemblies. Principal among these is the fare drum (numbered 11 in the drawing) which is made up of 202 individual components.

Conception

The Roadmap to Mechanisation

The year is 1945. It is twelve years after the London Passenger Transport Board (LPTB) was set up to integrate public transport in the Capital and in many respects London already has a modern and highly organised urban and suburban transport network. But anyone old enough riding on a bus, tram or trolleybus would notice that the ticket he or she was given had progressed little since the 1880s.

Few people perhaps will need introduction to the practice of using pre-printed tickets for passenger journeys issued by a conductor. Tickets are distinctive, even garish sometimes and issue is by means of inserting the ticket into an aperture in a ticket punch worn by the conductor, who depresses a lever on the front of the punch. A bell sounds and a small hole is punched in the ticket indicating the point to which the fare has been paid. The relevant information for the journey purchased, namely class of ticket, the various points along the route (which later came to be known as stage numbers), the sequential serial number of the ticket (for audit purposes) and, significantly, the value of the fare paid, all had to be pre-printed on the ticket.

Synonymous with the name of its principal exponent, the Bell Punch Company of Uxbridge, Middlesex, production and use of 'bell punch' tickets for use in London was on an industrial scale. A purpose built works in Effra Road, Brixton was established to cater for the ticket printing and distribution needs of London County Council Tramways; one of London Transport's larger constituent parts.

This works produced the 1.2 billion tickets required annually for London's tram and trolleybus operations but additional capacity had to be bought from the Bell Punch company for the 2.25 billion Central Bus, 266 million Country Bus and 25 million Green Line coach tickets needed every year.[1] Overall ticket printing costs in 1947 amounted to £99,000 for those sourced from Bell Punch and £36,000

Above: A common sight in the 1930s in London, although this view dates from May 1949, the bus conductor was the face passengers saw most, complete with Bell Punch, ticket rack and carrying box. Also known as ticket boxes, these were issued to conductors at the start of their duty by the garage traffic office (or output) staff and contained the punch machine, cleaning blade and spare ticket packs.
© TfL from the London Transport Museum collection

Above: Staff modelling new uniforms in 1941, both summer and winter versions and no doubt to utility specification. The use of Bell Punches suggests a bus setting although cancellers were generally not worn as per the photograph on page 9. It may indicate use on one of the relatively few Central Bus routes with sections common to tram and trolleybus operations which would require the use of cancellers to handle return tickets. Travel interchange arrangements such as these were one of the major barriers to the introduction of ticket machines in London.
© TfL from the London Transport Museum collection

for those printed at Effra Road (a total of £135,000 which in today's terms would be in the region of £5 million). In addition to road staff, the punch system was extremely 'back office' labour intensive with operatives known as 'Output Assistants' and based at Chiswick, Effra Road and at some decentralised locations such as Country Area garages, packing ticket boxes for each of the 12,371 duties performed annually by platform staff.[2]

On return, waybills were analysed to extract statistical information and reconcile paid in receipts with the value of unsold ticket stock. In the case of discrepancies and for audit purposes, punches had to be opened and the 'confetti' formed by the hundreds of holes punched in the ticket and retained within the machine laboriously hand counted. Overall in 1947 the cost of operating the punch ticket service for Central Buses alone was put at £176,000 (nearly £7 million in today's terms) of which approximately a third was labour, the remainder equipment, printing and establishment costs.[3]

But despite various Committees set up in the 1930s to explore the opportunities of mechanising ticket issue by the use of ticket machines that printed tickets on blank paper rolls, there had been a reluctance to change. This was partly due to very high standards of 'due diligence' in contemplating departure from a system that functioned dependably, as well as a less than satisfactory experience with those ticket machines inherited from constituent organisations in 1933. The main sticking point though was a complicated fares structure and the need for special fares and journey interchangeability which proved well beyond the capabilities of the relatively simple ticket machines thus far produced.

There was the need too for comprehensive statistical information to provide supporting evidence for fare increases to the Charges Consultative Committee and subsequently the transport tribunals set up in conjunction with the London Area Passenger Charges Scheme, established post-war by Attlee's Labour Government in an effort to introduce government control over public transport fares. Statistics had their use too for planning purposes to determine route details and journey frequency. By the use of conductors waybills completed at various stages of a bus's journey on its allotted route, it was possible to see what value of tickets were being issued (and therefore the extent of travel) and to whom (adult passengers, children, workmen etc). The system though wasn't perfect and proved to be extremely labour intensive. In pre-war days, this information was collected one week in every four but, due to austerity restrictions, this was cut back to one week only in summer and one in winter for the preparation of revenue estimates for the years 1940, 1944, 1946 and 1948 only.

The question of mechanising ticket issue on road services was considered by the Board's Ticket Committee meeting in December 1936 with the remit to "consider the number of services upon which ticket issuing machines could be introduced" and to report on "the difficulties which arise by reason of the Board's fare system in the universal adoption of these…machines".[4]

Of the machines inherited by the Board, the most numerous was the TIM. In July 1942, London Transport had 585 in use, dating from the period 1931 to 1933, used mainly on Central Buses (ex London General Omnibus Co. Ltd.) at its former garages at Clay Hall (123 machines) and Cricklewood (236). From fellow Underground Group company, London United Tramways, a further 168 were based at Fulwell and 50 at Isleworth for use on trolleybus services. Of the remainder, 7 were in use at Chelsham in the Country division and a solitary machine resided at the training school.

Limited to 9 fare values, the TIM was the only real player for urban bus operators wishing to mechanise in the pre-war period. Invented in about 1926 by a Frank Langdon, who worked at the time for the Neopost letter franking machines company, the TIM had in its favour simplicity and the speed of ticket issue, thanks largely to the means of selecting fares by use of a telephone-like dial on the machine bedplate. Indeed trials proved a TIM could issue a 1½d ticket without the need for giving change every 2.67 seconds while the equivalent punch ticket transaction took 3.56 seconds.[5]

The difference perhaps seems insignificant but, scaled up, the ability of a conductor to collect fares faster meant more fares could be collected. Uncollected fares were always a problem on busy central London routes, partly

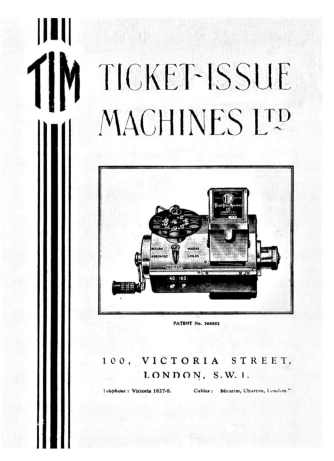

TICKET-ISSUE MACHINES LTD

PATENT No. 368803

100, VICTORIA STREET, LONDON, S.W.1.

Telephone: Victoria 1827-8.   Cables: "Micatim, Churton, London."

due to the sheer volume of passengers travelling but also the typically short nature of the journeys taken. Unless the conductor was quick, revenue would be lost and giving him or her the tools to do the job more efficiently had profound economic benefits.

The TIM machine was the market leader in the 1930s and London Transport inherited 600 at its formation. Illustrated is the sales booklet produced in the mid-1930s (reproduced by courtesy of Keith Edmondson), while the ticket left originated from one of the London Passenger Transport Board's constituent companies. To save the cost of having new ones made, the original company title was removed from the print plate and a block inserted printing 'L.P.T.B.' to the left of the stage number.

But there were other advantages to be gained from mechanisation. The use of blank paper rolls was considered to offer substantial savings in comparison to the laborious and expensive task of printing, sorting, securely storing and distributing pre-printed tickets with a monetary face value. The savings in back office costs alone would be considerable when a machine could be relied upon to work out the value of tickets sold by a simple comparison of starting and closing counter readings. Any 'shorts' or 'overs' would be immediately apparent. As it stood, resolving discrepancies relied on the rather protracted process of reconciling takings with unsold complete and partially used packs of tickets.

The real job of planning for London's mechanised fare collection requirements after the War brought about the setting up of the Ticket Machine Committee – Road Services in 1945 under the chair of B.H. Harbour, one of the Board's Commercial Managers. Earlier a design brief had been produced by Harbour for a suitable portable ticket machine: [6]
   a) Mindful of the need to carry the machine throughout a conductor's duty, it had to be light, a maximum of 3¼lb (1.5 kg) was recommended;
   b) It had to be simple to operate;
   c) It had to print and issue tickets rapidly and accurately;
   d) It had to record fares to the satisfaction of Board and conductor alike;
   e) Tickets produced from within the machine had to be legible to passengers, conductors and platform inspectors;
   f) It had to reduce to a minimum the duties of both conductor and back office staff in the processing of the machine for service and at duty end and in the handling and preparation of tickets and waybills.

In addition tickets had to show the following information:
   i. The ticket machine serial number;
   ii. A four digit sequential ticket serial number;
   iii. The fare paid in 14 separate denominations (i.e. 1d, 2d, 3d etc);
   iv. Class of ticket in 7 denominations (i.e. 'Ordinary', 'Child' etc);
   v. A two digit stage number;
   vi. A three digit route number;
   vii. The date of ticket issue;
   viii. The title 'LONDON TRANSPORT' and a summary of the conditions of issue.

A cancelling device embodied in the machine was required for dealing with return, transfer and pre-paid tickets which endorsed cancelled tickets with both the machine number and a four digit serial number which tallied with a register visible from the outside of the machine.

Additionally, the specification required a series of continuous registers visible externally that showed:
   1. The total number of tickets issued of each fare denomination;
   2. The total number of tickets issued (to enable reconciliation with 1. above);
   3. The total cash value of tickets issued in units of ½d and 1d or a total cash counter in £-s-d;
   4. The total number of cancelled tickets.
Ticket size was not to be smaller than 2' x 1' or in excess of 4' x 1¼'.

Rolls were to be of plain paper but it was permissible to have conditions of issue pre-printed. A minimum of 250 tickets would be obtained from a ticket roll and a visible warning given to the machine user in advance of the roll being exhausted. Rolls must be renewed easily by conductors without access to the working components of the machine.

The mechanism and registers were to be protected against accidental and fraudulent activation. The machine as a whole had to be free from sharp edges, have a polished and non-rusting outer casing, be rain and dust proof, capable of withstanding rough usage, require the minimum of inking, lubrication, setting and cleaning and offer a service life of at least 5 years.

No ticket issuing machine existed in 1945 that met all these requirements. The hope was that such a machine might be developed, in response prompting Harbour to circulate the specification to the relevant industry players including National Cash Registers Ltd and Bell Punch. Similarly advertisements were placed in the trade press. TIM Ltd was evidently not approached directly, given the existing relationship with that company and a wish, no doubt, to progress a little from "Langdon's machine" as a surviving hand written comment on file attested.

But subsequent reports from the Ticket Machine Committee and the Memoranda to the Executive Conference (The LPTB had become the London Transport Executive in 1948) highlighted some of the obstacles to overcome before comprehensively mechanised ticket issue on the streets of London could be achieved. Understandably, running two different ticketing systems (be they punch tickets or two different types of ticket machine) was seen as inefficient, confusing and potentially costly. But this was deemed necessary by the fares structure that applied in London and differing requirements of the three operating divisions.

With regard to fares, the August 1948 Executive Conference chaired by Lord Latham considered a report by J.H.F. Benford, London Transport Executive's Fares and Charges Officer that "the capacity of ticket machines with their fixed internal printing wheels would be less adaptable

to changes in fare scales than punch tickets that could be produced on a printing press to any value". Benford said tellingly to the Conference that full mechanisation "must await the reasonable certainty of a stabilisation of fares for a period of years, preferably on a scale of 1d jumps without intermediate ½d values".[7] The existence of ½d fares was compounded by the established practice of charging child fares at 50% of the equivalent adult fare. If child fares could be rounded up (or down) to the nearest 1d, and with it the elimination of intermediate ½d increments within the fare scale, then general fare increases would be much easier to accommodate within the constraints posed by machines with a fixed fare range. This was an important principle to understand and it is a point we shall return to with some regularity throughout our story.

Benford also identified the other main obstacle to a largely universal bus ticketing system for London's road transport, namely the very different character of the three

operating divisions. Central Buses, with its intense network of services in inner London and the immediate suburbs, had the lion's share of passenger numbers and perhaps offered the best opportunity to fully mechanise given a relatively compact fares structure and some shorter routes.

Theoretically the same could be said of the Trams and Trolleybuses division but here the difference was cultural. In the context of ticketing, as Benford put it in his 1948 report, "while the use of workmen's returns with inter-route transfer availability and general transfer system remains" then the brakes were being applied to a widespread use of ticket machines.

Above: In the post war period punch tickets remained the most widespread form of ticketing on surface transport in London. The conductor in this view is using an A type punch and canceller, both invented by George Gibson. © TfL from the London Transport Museum collection

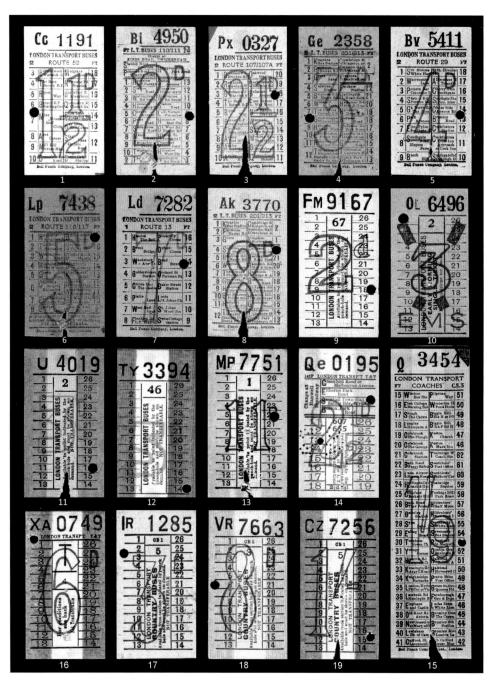

Left: Punch tickets kaleidoscope: 1-8; 'Geographical' Central buses issues, so called because fare stages are fully described on the ticket. 9-13; later these gave way to 'Numerical' style tickets where the same information is represented by a stage number showing the alighting point - 'EMS' stands for an 'Early Morning Single' issue, introduced in 1950. 14 & 16; Effra Road produced trolleybus tickets were of this distinctive type. 15; Green Line geographical ticket for route 704, 705 and 718. 17-19; Country Area issues, higher values were typically highly coloured for ease of recognition.

Below and right: Double issue Ultimate tickets reproduced to a larger scale, and the machine in use illustrated in a contemporary sales brochure.

The issue of special fares for workmen had political sensitivities surrounding it, embodied in the 'municipal socialism' of the late 19th century when many of London's publicly owned tramway systems were conceived. Early Morning Single (EMS) fares at special rates benefitting working people were introduced with the October 1950 fares revision in compensation for the withdrawal of Workman's Return fares on trolleybuses and trams (plus a few Central bus routes). The introduction of EMS fares, unlike the complexities of inter-route transferability, could be much more readily handled by a machine. It need only be equipped with a suitable class of ticket value making such issues readily identifiable.

Misgivings about abandoning interchangeability of travel on trams in particular was already fading as the trams themselves came to be replaced with trolleybuses, and after the War, with diesel engine buses. Other factors too were at play tilting the playing field more favourably toward the universal use of machines for fare collection in the post-war period. Firstly, abandonment of the strict principle of half adult fares for children was argued successfully to the various transport tribunals that met to agree proposed changes to the fares structure in the Capital, with the effect that at a stroke, this greatly reduced the number of increments in the fare scale. Secondly, general inflation had greatly reduced the buying power of the ½d coin to the extent that it needed to feature less and less in fare scales as Britain entered the 1950s.

The Country Bus network, and especially the long distance Green Line coach services, which had resumed after the wartime suspension, presented a rather different dilemma. Country services were generally longer and the range of fares wider so a machine with only a very limited range of fare values would struggle without excessive 'marrying up' of ticket issues. This problem was amplified for the coach network where high route mileage and fare values called for the use of a ticket machine with a much more extensive and flexible range of fare values.

The ticket machine industry in 1948
The post-war period was a busy one for the various manufacturers of ticket issuing equipment. This was due to the need of customers to re-equip after six years of war and to bring to fruition the various new designs that had been discretely in development while war related work took the limelight. The opportunity too was taken to improve

on existing designs. Those offering the most promise in comparison to the Board's 1945 specification to replace the punch system were:

Bell Punch Ultimate
Essentially the new Ultimate machine, which first appeared in 1946, was really only an automated ticket rack and instead of punching the tickets, they were ejected from the front of the machine from one of five, (or later) six, 'units' by depression of a lever. Double issues were possible when a button was pressed in conjunction with the operating lever which usefully doubled the fare range of the machine.

the most experienced conductor. But its principal downfall lay in the limited fare range; only 10 values even allowing for double issues, well below the 14 required in the London specification. This meant it was only suitable for short routes with low fares.

For this reason alone, the Ultimate was not a major contender for universal adoption to replace the punch system but it would nevertheless find a role later when a very different need arose, namely a suitable candidate for London's first generation of one person operated buses.

T.I.M.

An improved machine was introduced by Ticket Issuing Machines (TIM) of Love Lane, Cirencester, after the War, although heavier than its pre-war counterpart, it had the advantage of being more robust. In short range format, it bettered its 9 value forebear (which became known as the TIM9) with a machine capable of accommodating 12 fare values (the TIM12).

It has to be said London Transport was not unduly enamoured with the TIM. While it had served a useful purpose in the early 1930s, the design had not progressed very much and in the rigours of service life, the TIM9 on which experience of the type was based, had proved expensive to maintain; £2/17/0 in 1949, or over £100 per year per machine in today's terms.[8]

Examination of a TIM12 by London Transport's Signal Engineer, who tended to be called upon to add gravitas to the views of non-technical staff in reports for the Executive, concluded that the TIM12 was "fundamentally the same as the previous model" and "lightly built" with workmanship "not of a satisfactory standard". Similarly the use of die-cast components didn't find favour, particularly the all important cash register wheels that lacked the strength of steel or machined alloy. [9] Neither was the TIM12 particularly cheap. Excluding box and harness, the price of the standard machine was £35 in 1948 (over £1200 in today's terms), potentially more if bespoke features were added.

But in its favour it was a known quantity and, having separate counters for each fare value, it could produce the all important statistical analysis of ticket sales that was required. It had the backing too of a large company that was keen to attract London Transport's business. In comparison with the punch system, it was liked by the staff that used TIM machines, appreciating their speed and ease of handling. So much so, in fact, that the Executive found it expedient to

While the Ultimate could print the stage number boarded, everything else had to be pre-printed on the ticket. This raised the question of the additional costs associated with printed ticket rolls, which in the case of the Ultimate, had the added disadvantage of being perforated and hard to produce except on specialist printing machines.

In many respects though, Bell Punch had a winning design with the Ultimate. Simple, robust, reliable, and fast in operation, it pleased bus operators who wanted a 'no frills' approach. The trump card for Bell Punch was continued reliance on the company's core business of producing pre-printed ticket stocks. Naturally conservative in nature, the immediate post-war bus industry valued continuity in established practices and relationships and, as such, it became a firm favourite in the municipal public transport sector. So much so that it enabled Bell Punch to hold its ground in response to the growing threat posed by more progressive designs.

In terms of the 1945 specification, the Ultimate could deliver the required statistical analysis, albeit manually, much in the same way as the punch system had done. In field trials, the machine was certainly impressively quick. But it was also bulky and relatively heavy to carry. Reloading nearly spent ticket rolls involved attaching the start of the new roll to the end of the old one with sticky brown paper. On a 70 seat vehicle with a standing load at rush hour, this would have been a daunting task to even prolong the life of the increasingly decrepit and uneconomic fleet of machines inherited from the Underground Group rather than replace them with all that was to hand at the time, namely bell punches.

TIM's involvement didn't quite end there though and mention should be made of the long range TIM which offered the prospect of fares in 1d increments up to a maximum of 4/11½d which would have made it suitable for longer distance Country and coach routes. In the event this option wasn't seriously considered as by 1947 a more promising contender in the Setright 'Speed' or SM.B model had presented itself.

Setright 'Speed' or SM.B
Although London based at Hackney Wick, Setright Registers Ltd had not made significant inroads into operations in the Capital during the pre-war period with its 'Insert' model, which first appeared in 1929. Two of the smaller constituents absorbed by London Transport on the formation of the Board used them on express coach services, Premier Line Coaches

Opposite page: An Underground Group TIM9 from the early 1930s fitted with a guillotine that automatically cut the ticket on issue. © TfL from the London Transport Museum collection

This page: The Setright SM.B machine was briefly considered for use in central London, albeit in short range guise, but proved too slow in operation to be a serious contender. The illustration right, from a contemporary Setright brochure, shows the machine in long range guise.
The tickets illustrated below are from a Setright demonstrator (left) loaned to the Executive for evaluation purposes. The ticket class designation 'SINGLE' did not accord with London practice; 'ORD'Y' (for 'ordinary') was the accepted convention for all one journey machine issues as illustrated by the production machine version (right).

Prints from a roll

Left: One of the new Setright SM.B machines in service in August 1953 on Green Line route 721. In original format, Setrights were equipped with a full length insert as well as the smaller canceller slot in the front cover. As such, they would have been capable of validating Rover tickets. Concerns that inserting foreign matter into this slot could interfere with the way the fare value appeared on printed tickets, thus inviting fraud, led to the slot being plated over. © TfL from the London Transport Museum collection

Right: An early Insert Setright machine similar to those adopted by the LPTB in 1933. Used on Green Line routes at Grays and Romford, they were of two types; one issued tickets up to a maximum of 4/9d in 3d increments (ex Edward Hillman Ltd) while those taken over from Premier Line Coaches were of a more common type handling increases in 1d steps. Both used a cumulative cash register unlike the example illustrated.

and Edward Hillman Ltd, both so equipping with them the year before. The original Insert model was replaced by an updated machine in 1931, which in short range guise was known as the SR.D, followed in 1934 with a long range machine, the LR.D, capable of fares in 1d increments up to 11/11d. It was this machine that established Setright's reputation, with a sizeable following in the pre-war period amongst provincial bus operators, most notably the Walter Alexander & Sons empire in Scotland.

A total of 156 SR.D machines were inherited by the Board and remained in use on coach routes, focused on Grays and Romford garages, but were withdrawn with the curtailment of Green Line operations due to the War and not used again, their reputation evidently tarnished by their susceptibility to fraud.

The Insert Setright, as the name implies, relied on pre-printed tickets being manually inserted into an aperture in the front of the machine which printed the required information on the ticket such as fare paid, stage, date

etc. As such, it offered little real advantage over the punch system except in the back office process as receipts were recorded automatically by cash counters.

In the 1920s the Trambus, and later the Setright SM.A, were developed to offer customers a machine that printed tickets on plain paper rolls, but apart from small scale use by the London Public Omnibus Company until its takeover in 1929, the type was largely ignored except for a handful of operators.

This all changed with the appearance of a much improved model, the Setright SM.B, which did in part meet the 1945 ticket machine specification. It was available in two formats: a short range model giving all fares to 1/- in ½d increments and a long range machine offering the same capability but to a maximum fare of 12/11½d, later extended to 19/11½d. Moreover it was well engineered, impressively flexible in its ability to cope with a wide range of fare and class values and could even perform as a canceller with provision for an insert slot in the front casing; a throw back to the Insert model.

The Setright SM.B came to be widely adopted by provincial bus operators the length and breadth of Britain, and even made limited inroads into the municipal sector, the preserve of Bell Punch and TIM. But it had its limitations in the context of London Transport's needs. For a start, the machine had a relatively high purchase price (even in short range form, the SM.B cost £41/7/6 in 1950 (£1450 today) and there was the suspicion, subsequently born out by field tests, that it was quite a slow machine to use. The main drawback was that the SM.B lacked cash registers for each fare value, instead relying on a single cash-total register. This put it at a distinct disadvantage compared to both the TIM and the Ultimate.

The SM.B though did have the capability of recording statistical information for the numbers of tickets sold for any one pre-set fare and/or class value and up to two further classes of ticket issued. It couldn't combine both class and fare and identify, for example, all the 1/6d return tickets sold – only the sum of all the 1/6d tickets and the sum of all the return tickets, regardless of value. This did at least open up the possibility of limited statistical analysis by the sampling method.

Reporting in 1950, Benford remarked "the statistics register on the Setright worked well so the limited (cash) recording facilities of this machine cannot in themselves condemn its use" but concluded "with regard to the Setright, there are no counterveiling advantages to offset the substantial increase in expenditure due mainly to the high initial cost". Significantly his report identified the particular requirements of Green Line operations where the "issue is not speed of (ticket) issue but the ability to accommodate so many different types of ticket and value".[10]

Others were briefly considered as well, but dismissed as not practical. Principal among these 'also rans' was the Verometer machine, manufactured by Clayton-Harris of Lincoln. Principally

associated with the Birmingham & Midland Motor Omnibus Co. Ltd. ('Midland Red'), the machine had been tried in London experimentally in the 1930s. An improved post-war model was demonstrated but it was considered too heavy, bulky and slow to operate and lacked the necessary capability to deliver statistical analysis by fare value. It has to be said too, judging by the speed with which 'Midland Red' jettisoned their Verometers after taking a trial batch of Setright SM.Bs in 1949, this machine would not have been a successful choice in favour of the Gibson, to say the least.

For a variety of reasons, then, none of the proprietary ticket machines available was deemed wholly suitable for the job in hand but interestingly an alternative machine entirely developed from within London Transport itself, was already showing promise…

Birth

The first mention of "Mr Gibson's Ticket Machine" in the official record was in November 1944. In a memorandum to the Board's Solicitor General, A.H. Grainger, Fares and Charges Officer J.H.F. Benford refers to a ticket issuing machine, entirely the work of one man, that had been in development "for some years now" designed and built at the Board's Stockwell Road Punch Works. Evidently a working example had recently been completed and demonstrated to B.H. Harbour.[1] Until the matter of patenting the machine was dealt with though, there was no question at this stage it would see road use.

This comes as some surprise as there is no official reference hitherto that such a machine was being developed, or indeed existed. This may well have reflected the wartime conditions that still prevailed, when development work anticipating the War's successful outcome still had to be

Left: George Gibson pictured in April 1949, after he had retired, with a prototype machine, possibly C.B.1, as probably none of the new pre-production machines were sufficiently complete at that stage. The setting was Bowles Road Punch Works, as evident by the punches on the shelves behind.

Above: Various punches and cancellers invented by Gibson; the A type punch, of which approximately 9000 were made, is shown on the top row (middle and right). The bottom row are Gibson's cancellers for both the LCC and the LPTB, of which 7000 were made of all types. Cancellers were needed to mark tickets for a particular purpose with a distinctive signature consisting of, typically, a series of perforations that showed the canceller number. The 'pistol' punch shown in this official photograph, (top row, left) is typical of the type used in the late 19th century but has no known Gibson association. © TfL from the London Transport Museum collection

done discreetly, so as not to draw attention to materials and manpower being diverted away from essential war work. Indeed the machine shown to Harbour and approved by the General Managers Commercial Meeting of November 1944, may not have been the first to be built. Writing in 1988, Peter Brooks suggests the design was sufficiently advanced by 1942 for a prototype to be built "largely of brass" which would have been an easier task than construction from steel and aluminium alloy. It is likely a more substantial working example was constructed as well later and this may well have been the machine demonstrated to Harbour. [2]

It is at this point that the man credited with the invention of the machine that bears his name, enters the story. Born in 1877, George Gibson was one of 5 children, all but one boys, and spent his early years in Duns near Berwick upon Tweed in the Scottish borders. Educated at Paterson's Academy, Berwick, and at Berwickshire High School, George followed his father (also called George) into the family watch and clock making business situated at the corner of Hide Hill and Woolmarket in Berwick. In 1910 Gibson decided to travel south and took up employment that year with the London County Council Tramways (LCCT), subsequently becoming superintendent of the LCCT's Punch Works situated in Stockwell Road, Brixton. This works catered for the overhaul and repair of all the ticket punches and cancellers used by LCCT and its successor, London Transport. Drawing on his background as a watchmaker, Gibson showed promise as something of an inventor. He is responsible for devising and developing the ticket punch adopted by LCCT, known as the 'A type' punch of 1913, and also the ticket canceller introduced in 1910 that in improved form was adopted as standard throughout the system in 1935.

In post-war years, the Stockwell Punch Works would also have been tasked with keeping serviceable the aging TIMs and detailed knowledge of this machine, and its many fallibilities, may have prompted Gibson to design a ticket machine himself. Indeed it is said that the two machines have more features in common than separate them. Both operated on the principle of a circular 'print' drum' containing the type that prints the information on the ticket, which rotated 360° as the handle was turned. This drum came into contact with an ink impregnated roller and subsequently a rubber pressure roller that held the paper to be printed against the inked type. Both machines produced tickets on 1 and 7/16th inch wide paper which enabled the Gibson to utilise existing sources of ticket rolls. Where they principally differed is how the value of individual fare values were recorded. The TIM relied on a mutilated gear that moved transversely as the fare dial was turned and thus engaged the relevant fare value counter one or more times depending on the value selected. The susceptibility of those counters to damage, wear and abuse was one of the TIM's chief weaknesses. The Gibson used a very different and far more robust method, where all the fare value counters were compactly housed in a circular drum. On ticket issue, the relevant counter was actuated according to whatever fare value sat in the 12 o'clock position corresponding to the viewing window in the drum's external cover.

At this early stage of the machine's development, it seems certain there was no official sanction to what Gibson was doing and instead his eye was on the commercial potential for his invention. Many years before, in March 1920, he had assigned his rights under Letters Patent 16395/1913 for the A type punch to the Bell Punch company for which he was paid by them £500 (£22,500 today). An agreement for the punch was drawn up allowing LCCT to carry on using and manufacturing it without any royalty payments for their own operational use, but it allowed his invention to be marketed to outside operators for profit while at the same time protecting the rights of his employer, which jointly held the patent. In the event Bell Punch weren't interested in manufacturing the A type punch, after all they had a successful design already in production. The move was merely to exploit any technical advances it offered and prevent a rival company capitalising on it.

Provisional Letters Patent
Grainger was called upon to assist in patenting Gibson's ticket machine and advised that patent law required an individual be named as the patentee or joined with an employing organisation as joint patentee. The question arose too whether Gibson's earlier agreement with the Bell Punch company gave them any rights to the new machine. This was not thought to be a problem, as a covenant in the earlier agreement giving Bell Punch rights over "future improvements or development in punches" couldn't, it was thought, be applied to a machine capable of printing and issuing tickets. Moreover even if the argument was valid, the prevailing legal advice was that clauses in contracts could be overturned if "such an agreement could be considered an unreasonable constraint on trade". [3]

Matters were sufficiently advanced for the Board's patents agent, F.J. Cleveland & Co., to prepare a provisional patent specification by mid December 1944 and have it placed on file at the Patent Office by the end of that month. This protected the invention against anyone else patenting it for a period of 12 months to allow for a full specification to be prepared and drawings to be lodged with the Patent Office. It opened up the prospect of the production of a small number of machines for a limited service trial but there was no question of the Gibson machine being manufactured and entering large scale use until the full patent application could be made and duly approved.

This position was affirmed by Benford in a memorandum to Harbour in December 1944: "it would be unwise to take any step for production of this machine by outside firms until the patent questions have been settled". It would only be known once Letters Patent were granted "whether this machine has or has not infringed some existing patent...there are some hundreds of existing patents dealing with various types and designs of ticket issuing machines".[4]

With the provisional patent filed, the decision to proceed to Letters Patent had another obstacle to navigate, namely Board Organisational Circular No 6 issued in October 1939 which required any invention the Board intended to patent needing to satisfy the requirement that "its major purpose (being) to simplify the construction and maintenance of the machine compared with the known types of (other) ticket issuing machines". Benford went on to explain "while the new machine does not purport to revolutionise mechanical ticket issuing, it is considered that its simplicity of construction and the arrangement of the working parts represent a substantial advance towards reliability and should result in considerable economies in maintenance costs"[5] In other words, the Board only had the necessary authority to apply for the patent in so far as it met a need relevant to the Board's activities and only in the absence of that need being met by a suitable proprietary alternative. The proposed Gibson patent was deemed to clear this hurdle and the path ahead lay clear to the full patent application being made.

In the same memorandum Benford goes on to say '"Mr Gibson was enabled to evolve the invention by virtue of his employment with the Board but he was not required to do so". In consideration for his work, Benford proposed "a sum of £250 be paid to Mr Gibson in respect of the design of the machine now covered by Provisional Patent 25938/44 and further, that in respect of licences or royalty payments for machines of this type other than those required by the Board, Mr Gibson should not be asked to assign his rights to the Board, but should be free to make his own terms and to himself receive any royalty payments in respect of machines manufactured other than those required by the Board which should, of course, be free of royalty payments".

While Benford and the Commercial Managers B.H. Harbour and T.E. Thomas were agreed on Gibson's package, which seemed fair reward for his efforts and not

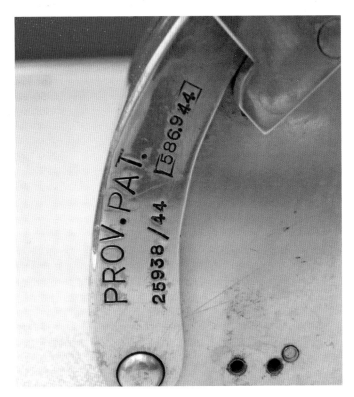

employment and if ever there was a case where a device was the result of constant association in handling these machines, I should have thought that this was one where the Board should share with the patentees the proceeds of any sale or royalties".[6] The matter was allowed to rest there and Gibson was permitted to profit from his invention commercially, but had the outcome been different, the Gibson machine may not have been manufactured for use outside London. This may well have made the whole business of attracting a suitable commercial partner to build the machine all the more difficult and expensive.

Amid the celebrations of May 1945 that the War in Europe was finally over, a formal Heads of Agreement was signed between Gibson and the Board. It left Gibson free to profit from his invention by its sale to outside parties and, if he so wished, to sell his share of any Letters Patent or to grant exclusive or non-exclusive licences for the machine to be manufactured "subject to the approval of the Board" to which Gibson himself added "which approval shall not be unreasonably withheld". The Board retained its right to manufacture or have manufactured the machine for its own use free of any encumbrance. Moreover, the Board protected its position in the event Gibson sold his interest

unduly generous given what he had made out of the deal 25 years before with Bell Punch, nevertheless there was an objection to the Board not sharing in the wider commercial appeal of the machine. Benford was obliged to stand his ground when the decision was challenged by C.G. Page, the Board's Secretary who wrote in March 1945 "I assume that this is your final decision that must stand but I must say that I think that it is an unfortunate precedent to create as there are others who develop patents during the course of their

Opposite page and this page: The earliest surviving Gibson machine is C.B.1 which is housed in the London Transport Museum artefacts collection at Acton.

Inset: A ticket issued on 25th June 1945 when machine 11, one of the original trio of 10 fare value Gibsons, was in trial use on trolleybus route 604 from Fulwell depot.

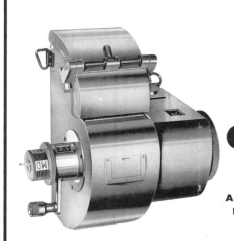

THE
GIBSON
A14
AUTOMATIC TICKET
ISSUING MACHINE

by

Crawley Ticket Machines Ltd.

This page and opposite bottom: More views of C.B.1 in the Museum collection. The fare drum and cover was smaller than in the production machine having a capability of recording only ten fare values, which was considered perfectly adequate at the time when the TIM9 machine was limited to only nine. Something of a fare values 'arms race' was sparked off by introduction of TIM's new post-war machine which had 12 fare values. In response the Gibson was redesigned to incorporate 14.

Opposite top: The 'spade' type of harness attachment on the back of the prototype machines was intended to engage a pocket in a strengthened leather apron in conjunction with a conventional leather strap worn over the right shoulder. This arrangement was carried over to the pre-production batch but proved unsatisfactory in prolonged use.

Above and right: Contemporary advertising material from Crawley Ticket Machines, which had purchased George Gibson's share of the patent. The lack of a suitable demonstrator meant C.B.1, with only ten values, had to be photographed to illustrate the brochure which clearly referred to the availability of a 14 fare value machine.

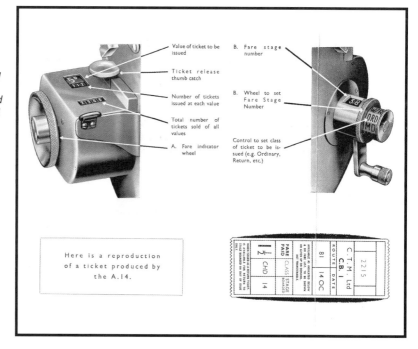

Value of ticket to be issued

Ticket release thumb catch

Number of tickets issued at each value

Total number of tickets sold of all values

A. Fare indicator wheel

B. Fare stage number

B. Wheel to set Fare Stage Number

Control to set class of ticket to be issued (e.g. Ordinary, Return, etc.)

Here is a reproduction of a ticket produced by the A.14.

The first service trial

Even before the provisional patent had been lodged, thought turned to how the machine might be produced in quantity if it proved successful. Somewhat prematurely, Benford even considered possible partner firms to develop and produce the machine.

These included Bracknell, Munro and Rogers Ltd of Bristol which designed and built the Board's change giving and automatic ticket machines in use on the Underground. The respected name of the Westinghouse Brake and Signal Co. Ltd. of Chippenham, Wilts, was another possibility. They had built the rapid ticket printers also used by the Railway Division and would go on to market the German built AEG portable ticket machine known as the 'Omniprinter', much favoured by British Railways in later life.

And the familiar name of Bell Punch appears too on his list. Benford rather cryptically notes in his memorandum to Harbour that "in view however of their very substantial interests in ticket printing, they might find themselves in some difficulty in being asked to develop and manufacture a machine designed to issue tickets from blank rolls".

in the machine by a clause limiting the price charged to the Board of machines bought or hired from the purchaser of Gibson's patent "not to exceed the prevailing prices charged by the purchaser to other customers less any royalty which would be included for the reservation of the right of the LPTB for free manufacture or use".[7]

What can be taken from all this is that firstly, Gibson probably had very little input from others to get to the stage of producing a working prototype. Had this been a team effort then the freedoms this arrangement gave him would not have been so forthcoming. Secondly, although the London Passenger Transport Board would greatly benefit from his invention, other than employing Gibson in the field of maintaining ticket equipment, his job description didn't require him to produce new designs of machines. He acted purely on initiative. And finally, while understandably wishing to protect its own business interests, London Transport can be seen acting as an enlightened public body in not standing in the way of commercial enterprise.

The firm of Hall Telephone Accessories (1928) Ltd was another name on Benford's list and laid claim to the Autographic machine as well as being a respected manufacturer of self service ticket dispensing machines.

TIM Ltd was notably absent though and Benford remarks "one of the essentials of producing such a machine...will be to ensure that the workmanship and materials are of the first quality so as to avoid the high maintenance and replacement costs we have experienced". [8]

Notwithstanding the need to obtain Letters Patent, a service trial was necessary to establish if 'Mr Gibson's ticket machine' would pass muster in the unforgiving world of day in day out operational use. Harbour initially proposed approaching the Monotype Corporation to build 12 prototype machines to Gibson's design, but in December 1944 Britain was still at war and this proposal was scaled back to 6. Subsequently this became only 3 which was considered within the capacity of the Punch Works to fabricate themselves, without adversely affecting the business of servicing and repairing ticket punches and cancellers.

These three early examples, built at Stockwell in the late spring and early summer of 1945, were numbered 10, 11 and 12 and at this stage still had only 10 fare values (1d, 1½d, 2d, 3d, 4d, 5d, 6d, 7d, 8d and 9d). There were significant differences to later manifestations of the machine in the means of activation of the fare drum counters, as well as a different type arrangement for the print drum. In other respects though they looked very similar to the eventual production Gibson.

Remarkably a 10-fare prototype machine survives in the possession of the London Transport Museum Depot reserve collection at Acton (item 1985/106). The exact provenance of this machine is unclear, however, as it carries a later patent number referring to a modified design and is numbered C.B. (presumably standing for Central Buses) No 1. Evidently this machine was used as a demonstrator when the Gibson entered commercial production some years later, as it appears in advertising literature of the time. Whether it be one of the original batch of three (albeit in modified form) or a later incarnation, isn't known. Certainly the fare range of C.B.1 accords with the three trial machines but it has different classes of ticket values: 'C' (child) for example as opposed to 'MDC' (mid-day child) characteristic of the machines used for the trial.

Siemens Bros & Co. Ltd were put forward too as potential partners: manufacturers of telephone exchange and railway signalling equipment, the parent German company had developed in pre-war years the advanced and compact Autowaybill machine tested operationally in Leeds.

Above: The well known firm of Siemens Bros. & Co. Ltd. offered the Autowaybill ticket machine to the transport industry in the 1930s but was better known to the LPTB as electrical engineers, with a large manufacturing site in Woolwich.

Experimental use with these three 10-fare Gibsons began on 8th August 1945 with machine 11 despatched to Fulwell depot. No 12 followed on 3rd September 1945 for use at Cricklewood and No 10 appeared three days later at Reigate. This pattern established the principle for subsequent trials that the machines should be tested on each of the three operating divisions: Trams and Trolleybuses, Central Buses and Country Buses, to gather as varied an experience as possible of different operational environments. The choice of locations was also significant as two were established TIM users. This allowed a more objective appraisal to be made by staff already experienced in using ticket machines.

Staff reaction was generally very positive, mostly detail around the unsatisfactory harness arrangement for carrying the machine and a problem with tickets 'concertinaring' due to the poor quality paper used for the ticket rolls or, more likely, inexperienced conductors not cleanly tearing off the ticket on issue. This had the affect of allowing paper fragments to remain in the machine impeding emergence of the next ticket. Conductor Hanson (4411) from Fulwell commented "I am sure it is far superior to the TIM" although several comments referred to the fact it was heavier; 4lb 3oz compared to the TIM's 3lb 6oz. The knob selecting the class of ticket evidently only turned in one direction which was somewhat irksome but hardly of major concern. [9]

Another quirk of this early machine, subsequently corrected when the type plate was redesigned, was that the portion of the ticket carrying the date was retained within the machine to form part of the next ticket issued, so the first ticket of the day invariably carried the wrong date. This is a familiar characteristic of the much later Almex A machine when a 'no value' ticket had to be issued to allow the wrongly dated ticket to pass through. For the Gibson, tickets of no value were not a possibility.

A common feature of Gibson usage by the Country Buses division was the issue of tickets with no route number; the print wheels being set to '000'. This was largely because a duty could involve use on more than one route and it wasn't reasonable to expect platform staff to change the route number details printed on the ticket themselves (which involved a special stylus and was the responsibility of office staff). This trend continued throughout Gibson use in the Country Area and for that matter it also became a feature of Gibson operations on trolleybuses, for much the same reason. However, judging by ticket evidence, this is by no means universally the case and route numbers do appear on some country and trolleybus tickets.

During the trial, staff used to the TIM missed the reset facility that allowed the fare dial to return to the lowest (and most issued) value with a simple flick of a finger. It has to be said the TIM bettered the Gibson for speed of issue generally as potentially the Gibson fare selector knob would have to be rotated up to 180° between consecutive tickets with significantly differing fare values.

The trial lasted until 2nd November 1945 and during that time machine '10' at Reigate had issued 27,902 tickets, '11' (Fulwell) the most at 53,804 and '12' at Cricklewood, 24,180. The various divisional managers submitted their reports to Harbour and the results were considered "very satisfactory" with no incidences of breakdowns. In Harbour's words, "most considered it to be smoother, sturdier and easy to operate"[10] and "a better constructed machine than the TIM with the mechanism inaccessible without the need for special tools". [11]

Application for full Letters Patent was duly made on 18th December 1945, with the expectation that preparation could now begin in earnest to phase out the Board's reliance on pre-printed tickets for road operations. This was predicated on granting of full Letters Patent, a process expected to take 12 months because of a backlog at the Patent Office due to the War. In the event, this estimation proved to be well wide of the mark.

Coming of Age

Patent problems

In the final months before his retirement from London Transport in May 1946, Gibson was working on an improved design for his machine. In a handwritten memorandum to Benford he set out a new method for actuating the fare drum counters by means of a three pronged cam directly driven by the fare drum assembly. The earlier design had relied on an intermediate gear. Gibson wrote "the improvement on this machine I have made since it was patented should in my opinion be protected. It would strengthen the existing patent. If machines were produced in quantity, a saving of approximately 15/- on each machine would be effected".[1] The new parts could be made as stampings, far cheaper than the relatively expensive business of producing gears that each had to be individually machined.

This was in many regards a positive development but it had the unfortunate effect of delaying getting the machine produced while the necessary patenting fall-out was resolved. Cleveland & Co. was consulted, and in their opinion, the new arrangement for driving the fare drum counters needed protection by application for a Patent of Addition to 25938/44 (the pre-existing patent application). At least this meant the pre-existing application could be utilised rather than starting again and no additional annual patent renewal fee had to be paid.[2] Patent of Addition was subsequently filed on 12th July 1946 as 20959/46. Another period of waiting ensued and what at the start had seemed a fairly straightforward business was becoming bogged down, due to the Patent Office clearly struggling to deal with work that was rapidly building up as British industry, eager to modernise, returned to peacetime activities.

If London Transport's management had been tempted to start to produce the machine in any number prior to obtaining Letters Patent, they would have been put off this idea by a letter received in September 1946 from an unlikely source. This was a firm called C. Ades Ltd, a Ford concessionaire

Left: A June 1946 view of one of the three 1945 prototype machines modified to accept the 14 value fare drum. In this case it was evaluated on trolleybus route 604 from Fulwell depot but it also did stints at Cricklewood and Nunhead garages. © TfL from the London Transport Museum collection

based in Baghdad, Iraq. The letter inquired if the Gibson machine was available for export. This set alarm bells ringing at 55 Broadway: the existence of the Gibson machine was clearly becoming common knowledge to the outside world. Had it been used extensively in service without patent protection, and it could be established that the design breached a patent someone else held, the Board could be liable for damages with the likely outcome that the whole mechanisation programme would be derailed.

The response from the Patent Office Examiner had to wait until December 1946 when, in his opinion, six pre-existing patents made claim or partly made claim to certain aspects of Gibson's 1944 patent:

- 368,802 Langdon
- 349,014 Fahrkartendrucker
- 305,682 Bethel
- 185,770 Ellis
- 27797/11 Meyer
- 3469/07 Ohmer

Amendments were duly made to the specification to overcome the similarities with other patents and a revised application was lodged with the Patent Office in February 1947. The changes were only minor and the overall design of the machine remained much as before, but it was another unwelcome delay. Finally, on 8th April 1947, Letters Patent for 25938/44 were issued in the joint names of George Gibson and the London Passenger Transport Board and, subject to payment of the annual renewal fee of £5, patent protection would remain in place until 18th December 1961.

Certainly a major step forward, but this still left outstanding the Patent of Addition and another obstacle presented itself in July 1947, when the Patent Office were advised that TIM Ltd intended to submit notice of opposition to the granting of the original patent. In response, the Patent Office agreed to a request by TIM's lawyers for an extension to the normal period of 1 month for objections to the granting of Letters Patent. No records exist to throw light on the frank exchanges of views that were no doubt taking place between Benford and M.W. Ingram, TIM Ltd.'s Managing Director. But the outcome was that nothing was

forthcoming from TIM by the cut off date a month later and the matter was quietly allowed to lapse. This may have been a delaying tactic only and no doubt TIM Ltd still had occasion to view the Board as a potential customer, with some good reason.

Matters were finally concluded with the issue of Letters Patent for 20959/46 (the fare drum counter modification) on 14th December 1948, still in joint names of George Gibson although the co-patentee was now the British Transport

Above: Another view from the 1946 trial—the conductor is using a small canceller attached to the strap of his harness of a type more commonly associated with the TIM machine. © TfL from the London Transport Museum collection

Commission following the London Passenger Transport Board coming under the aegis of the Commission to become the London Transport Executive on 1st January 1948. Belatedly, with the patent issue resolved, this opened the door to getting the machine into production.

More service trials

At a time of rapid technological advances, London Transport had an impressively orderly and systematic approach to adopting new products, which was based on a careful appraisal of their quality of design, construction and applicability to the allotted task. Whether or not it passed muster involved subjecting the new product to thorough testing in field trials where data would be systematically collected and analysed. While the earlier Gibson trial in 1945 had been successful, two months use with only three machines was not considered a sufficiently firm base to commit the Executive to the adoption of a still largely untried machine for the lion's share of its fare collection needs. In matters of revenue generation, it comes as little surprise that the stakes were extremely high. Although it offered promise, the Gibson was still an unknown quantity.

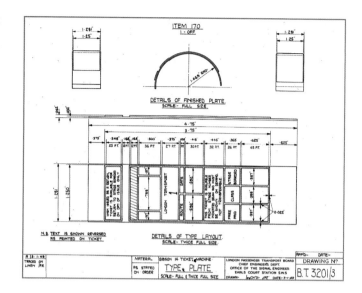

A substantial advancement had been made, while the patent issue was being resolved, by enlarging the machine's fare drum (and the outer casing to house it) so that it could now accommodate an additional 4 counters, making up the desired total of 14 fare values. This meant that of all the contenders, it came closest to the 1945 specification and was able to handle the entire Central Area fare range in use at that time. Gibson himself no doubt anticipated this improvement before his retirement, but equally his successor at the punch works, Charles Speller, may well deserve much of the credit.

Left: The same occasion as the picture on page 20; the man next to George Gibson is his successor, Charles Speller, who needs to be credited with much of the later design work and getting the Gibson into service. © TfL from the London Transport Museum collection

Above: A drawing produced by the Signal Engineer's Office for the design of the type plate for the pre-production batch of machines. It indicates the numbering sequence began at '1'.

Right page: The predominant use of alloy marks out the pre-production machines externally from the final specification as this view of No 58 illustrates. The ticket it produced is closer to what became the final format than those issued by the three 1945 prototype machines.

A prototype 14 value machine, likely modified from one of the ten value participants in the 1945 trial, was inspected by the Ticket Machine Committee in March 1946. The intention was to test this new machine in service for 3 week stints on each of the two inner London operating divisions and for 2 weeks in the Country Area. We know for certain it worked at Cricklewood and Nunhead in April and May 1946 respectively, alongside a new TIM12 loaned for the purpose, and was used also on trolleybus route 604 on 25th June 1946, as the occasion was photographed for publicity purposes. This was a relatively low key affair though and really only an extension of bench testing the new design features and gauging staff reaction. At the same time the Signal Engineer was asked for his views on this improved machine and in his opinion it "showed that the design and construction were extremely good. No wear whatever could be seen on any of the parts. The mechanism can be maintained quite easily and all points where wear would take place have been given special attention".[3]

Field trials were undertaken in November 1946 to assess the speed of issue of the various ticket machines in contention at the time and one of the 10-fare value Gibson variants was used alongside an Ultimate on loan from Bell Punch. The result was that the Ultimate won hands down on speed at 1.72 seconds per transaction where no change was required while the Gibson at 2.67 seconds was slower than the TIM, but significantly quicker than a punch (3.56 seconds).[4] This had not been the first trial with an Ultimate: four machines had apparently been tried in March 1946 on routes 85 and 63.

An Audit Office report of June 1948 looked at the likely cost implications of adopting either the Gibson or TIM machine compared to the punch system for Central Buses operations. Equipment costs for covering all the 12,371 daily weekday duties were £137,690 for punches but rose significantly to £329,687 (£13 million in today's terms) for adopting the Gibson and £453,397 for the TIM12. Annual running costs were put at £176,000

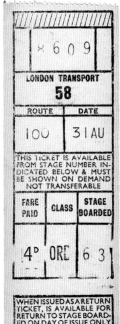

(punch – reflecting the high cost of producing the tickets), £153,000 (£6 million today) (Gibson) and £168,000 (TIM12). The Gibson was thought to be the cheaper of the two ticket machines to operate because of lower establishment costs.

With the patent issue out of the way, a large scale trial with 60 Gibson 14 machines was approved in August 1948 and this would run in conjunction with a more limited experiment with 25 Ultimates and 3 of the new short range Setright SM.Bs on loan.[5]

Firstly, sufficient Gibsons had to be built for the trial. Approval from the Executive in the form of Special Expenditure Requisition (SER 21/2011) was obtained and at an agreed budget of £2400, which equated to £40 (£1500 today) per machine. In the event this budget was wholly inadequate for the task in hand, largely due to unanticipated increases in materials costs, as much as 300% in some instances, and a minimum order requirement of 100 items from

many of the component suppliers. The cost of producing a detailed set of drawings, which still survive, undertaken by the Signal Engineer's Office at Earl's Court, wasn't factored in either. In the end the final bill to construct these 60 machines was £4425 or £73/14/6 (£2600 today) apiece, more than twice the cost of a TIM12.

The overspend had to be reported to the Executive with some degree of discomfort one detects in reading the reports from David McKenna, the Commercial Manager overseeing the project. The machines were paid for out of the Revenue Account rather than a Suspense Account set up for the purpose and there is evidence too of some 'creative accountancy' in the way the value of the excess stock of components bought in (£994/3/0) was assigned to 'spare parts stock'. The short service life of the trial machines hardly justified carrying such an extensive stock of parts although some, but not all, of these unused components were later utilised for building the production machine.

Today these 60 early machines are known as the 'pre-production Gibson' and there were some detailed differences that set them apart from the familiar and ubiquitous machine that followed. The outer casing was in polished alloy rather than the satinised finish adopted later. The handle knob and fare and class change knob were alloy too and the print drum cover extended in a graceful arc ending in a point, rather than the flat bottom arrangement of subsequent machines. An aperture was provided in the machine's exterior casing to apply ink to the fibre rollers, 2 rather than the single roller adopted later.

The service trial began in late November 1949 when 30 of the batch of 60 Gibsons were complete and ready to be set to work on route 1 from Cricklewood garage, where the earlier Gibson trial had centred. Shortly afterwards, the 25 Ultimate machines began work on route 128 from Enfield garage, moving to route 67 in April 1949 and subsequently route 125. The remaining Gibsons were earmarked for use

What's in a number…

Speculation exists as to the exact number of pre-production machines produced. There is a reference in an Audit Office report of 18th May 1950 valuing the surplus materials after construction of 61 machines; i.e. one more than the authorised build run of 60. Indeed, examining surviving ticket evidence, the highest numbered pre-production machine would appear to be 65. Were it not for ticket evidence that clearly shows the existence of machine No.1, this might have suggested the numbering sequence began at No.5.

A likely explanation for ostensibly pre-production machines with numbers greater than 60 (or 61 if indeed that number were built) may lay in the subsequent use of unused materials from the earlier batch finding their way to what, by then, were very early trial production machines. We do know that in 1951, 15 unused type plates were sold to the company that went on to manufacture the Gibson

machine and these presumably would have been in sequence with the 61 pre-production machines. Examining the plans drawn up in 1949 for the pre-production machine by the Signal Engineers Office, the type plate drawing clearly shows it bearing the number '1', implying this was the first of the series. I think this is one of those occasions where we will never really know the true answer – my own feeling is that only 60 or 61 were built and the higher numbers are explained by the subsequent use of these plates on later machines – after all the cost of producing them was 21/- each – it is doubtful in times of post war shortages, valuable items such as these would have been discarded simply because they bore a non-sequential machine number. Notwithstanding this, the first production machine officially began a new numbering sequence at '101' (as illustrated on page 41).

Above: This well known publicity view from 1951 shows pre-production machine No 33 with some amended features which were adopted for the production machine. Notable is the flat base to the casing, principally to save weight, but it had the advantage too that it could be placed upright on a flat surface. Not apparent in this view is the ebonite finger grip to the handle and a different design of fare selector, still in alloy but with indentations to the knurled outer rim. The harness now consisted of webbing to allay staff concerns over the weight of the new machine, but still with only two straps, not the four later adopted. © TfL from the London Transport Museum collection

Left: Three generations of Gibson machines — the nearest, a production variant; next to it, a pre-production machine and farthest, C.B.1. The most apparent differences are the greater use of moulded parts and the evolving shape of the casing.

on a trolleybus route (20 machines) and for the Country Area (10). On delivery in January 1950, Fulwell was again chosen as the receiving trolleybus depot. Representing the Country Area, predictably Reigate was selected first for use on service 406, examples too found their way to Staines and East Grinstead. The allocation to Reigate later swelled to 21 machines with only 10 at Fulwell, so there was clearly some fluidity in the allocation. The April 1951 ticket machine allocation data shows 6 remaining in use on Central Area buses, 6 with Country buses at Staines and the balance of 49 in store at the Stockwell Punch Works.

As for the Setright SM.Bs, these arrived in July 1949 for use on Central Buses route 14 and overall the trial continued with all three types of machine in use until March 1950 although, as we saw above, some Gibsons lingered until 1951.

Sufficient operational experience and data had been obtained from the pre-production Gibson trial by the late Spring of 1950 for the results to be put to the Executive for a decision that would decide London's bus ticketing requirements for a generation. It was decided though that the imminent Transport Tribunal deliberations in accordance with the London Area Passenger Charges Scheme, due to convene in May 1950, should take precedence. As L.C. Hawkins, from the Office of the Executive, commented in reference to Benford's preoccupation with the fares matter, "this is obviously a case where the quality of the report is more important than the speed of its preparation". [6]

The promised report wasn't forthcoming until September 1950. It reminded the Executive that 21,000 ticket machines would be required to equip all the duties operated by Central Road Services and Country Buses. The speed trial results were set out in the report, demonstrating the Gibson machine proved to be 17% faster in collecting fares than the use of punch tickets where change was required and impressively 25% quicker without the need for change. The gap was narrower for Country Buses, reflecting the need for double issue tickets because of longer distances travelled and higher fares. [7]

In terms of cost, at an estimated procurement cost of £76,000 per 1000 machines for the Gibson, this was only bettered by the Ultimate, but the estimated cost of £37,900 to keep these 1000 machines supplied with tickets for a year more than made up for the difference. Overall the Ultimate would be £55,600 more expensive. In conclusion, the report rather predictably identified the only practical choice as between the TIM12 and the Gibson 14 – the Ultimate was

dismissed for its limited fare range while the Setright lacked the necessary statistical capability and proved the most expensive to buy.

But what really clinched it in the Gibson's favour in comparison with the TIM was an unbeatable cocktail of lower costs, greater flexibility in accommodating 14 fare values and better design and execution. And so it was that London Transport's bus ticketing requirements were decided upon for what was predicted to be a horizon of 15 to 20 years and, while it could not have been foreseen at the time, this of course turned out to be far longer.

As for the runners up, the TIM12 would have the consolation of being selected to provide a stop gap to overcome the hiatus created while a manufacturing base for the Gibson was being established. With regard to the others, London Transport was sufficiently impressed with the Ultimate to later adopt it for the first generation of one-person-operated buses while 580 Setright machines, in long range form, had a long and successful life equipping Green Line coaches.

Before we leave the 1949/50 trial, worthy of mention is staff reaction to the new Gibson and it has to be said that, to the Executive's credit, the gathering of such opinions was no empty exercise. Staff reactions were taken seriously in an industry increasingly sensitive to labour relations and modifications were indeed made to make the work of the conductor as easy as possible. While evidently nothing had been learnt from the earlier trial about the unsatisfactory 'spade' arrangement to carry the machine, especially bearing in mind the additional weight when compared to the TIM9, a panel of experts was set up to develop a suitable harness. Efforts were made also to lighten the machine. When a conductor at Cricklewood had her tunic ruined by a leakage of indelible ink, the inking aperture was deleted for the production variant of the machine which instead relied on a pressure saturated roller that was externally inaccessible and renewed at overhaul. The problem of paper crumpling up in the machine reoccurred during the trial and this directly lead to the ticket roll housing being redesigned.

The reaction of conductors at Reigate was particularly interesting as here Gibsons were used in lieu of punches and ticket racks. Conductor Giles talked of "dirty hands" while using his Gibson but in spite of investigation, there was no evidence that the machine had been responsible for this. Conductor Goacher found the machine bulky and tended to obstruct passengers boarding and alighting from the bus, especially in overcoats. Conductor Harding was allocated machine No 46 and he had trouble reading the fare value as the drum didn't correctly align in the window. [8]

Overall though 95% of staff opinion was positive at Reigate and the 'both hands free' method of collecting fares and the ease with which a ticket roll could be changed, both struck a chord. Reactions from staff hitherto using TIMs were more muted and comparisons based on both weight and speed were considered to be backward steps. Tests undertaken to establish whether Gibson usage could improve takings (one of the principal tenets of why mechanisation was taking place) proved disappointingly elusive. Summing up in his report to the Executive, Benford concluded "the Gibson machine should be adopted as the future standard".

At the time, the Gibson could cover all the fares in the Central Area scale up to 10d in whole pence, except 6d and 7d, which required combination of lower fare values in the form of a 'double issue' linked by the COM or combination class value. The main caveat in his report was that the Gibson lacked flexibility in the face of future fare revisions without the need to make internal alterations to the machine, in particular those involving ½d fare graduations beyond the 1½d fare then still in use. But the Gibson had earned its spurs and attention could now turn to getting approval for bulk production.

Punch reprieve and the TIM12

In spite of the promise the Gibson machine was showing, the slow rate of progress to mechanisation was becoming of concern. A more pressing matter also presented itself; the desperate need to replace the pre-war TIM9 machines, some of which were approaching 20 years old.

With some reluctance it has to be said, the only viable contender to plug the gap until the production Gibson would be ready, which realistically was not going to be before 1952, was to purchase 1000 TIM12 machines. At an informal Road Services meeting in December 1949, chaired by A.B.B. Valentine of the Executive, and a future Chairman of London Transport, it was minuted, "that although the staff make complaints of TIM machines, they are unwilling to accept Bell Punches instead". [9]

The post-war TIM12 was an improvement on its 1930s counterpart and one was tried informally in April 1946 in service at Cricklewood and the following month at Nunhead garage alongside the prototype Gibson 14. Staff reaction was more in favour of the Gibson but B.H. Quinn, the District Superintendent at Cricklewood commented, "the new TIM is an improvement on the old type being generally a good tool apart from mechanical trouble…it was repaired on both occasions by TIMs at Cirencester". [10]

Sensing perhaps some hesitation on behalf of the Executive to buy more TIM machines, but lured by a marketing scoop if they did, Managing Director M.W. Ingram and TIM Ltd.'s Sales Director D.H. Kinnard approached Benford with a very tempting proposition. What was on offer essentially was a 'hire purchase' deal whereby the Executive could buy the machines without capital outlay by agreeing

Above: The TIM made an unexpected, and in some quarters unwelcome, return to London service in 1950 in the form of the TIM12, when the anticipated introduction of Gibson machines stalled. Ironically many were used to replace existing decrepit TIM9 ticket machines, not as was hoped, to sweep aside the use of ticket punches.

to pay an enhanced price if they took the paper ticket rolls from TIM. This would be at the cost of £48 per machine that would come with 3000 ticket rolls (which would last approximately 5 years), thereafter the machines would be solely the property of the Executive. Benford remarked "the offer of the TIM company seems to me to be attractive... both in respect of the machines and the paper supplies ... and I would recommend purchase (by that means) of 1000 machines". Someone at 55 Broadway evidently did the maths and compared to the outright purchase price plus the cost of buying in the ticket rolls, the saving per machine in acquiring it was about £1. [11]

Clearly in Benford's mind at the time was not only replacement of the surviving 549 TIM9s, but the imminent closure of the tram system. He was under pressure too from J.B. Burnell, the Central Road Services Operating Manager who commented "as a matter of expediency, the TIM company's offer should be accepted".

So it was then that 1000 TIM12 machines formed the first major phase of London Transport's post-war fare collection mechanisation programme. As it turned out, a more conventional means of financing the deal was agreed with outright purchase of each machine for a discounted price of £29/10/0, leaving the field clear to obtain the rolls elsewhere.[12] TIM also agreed to make some modest modifications to the machines to meet the Executive's requirements and moreover undertook to fulfil the order by the middle of 1951. Creditably, all were in service by the close of December 1950 and allocated to Cricklewood (390), Victoria (243) and Camberwell (291) supplanting either TIM9s or the use of punch tickets. The remainder of the batch were sent to Hackney (68 in total for route 22 only) and a small allocation of 4 to Alperton for Wembley Stadium specials. The Commercial Managers retained one intended for Audit Office use in the event possible fraud investigations required reference to a suitable machine and 3 resided at the Chiswick training school.

A new partnership is born

In May 1949 Gibson wrote to Benford informing him he had sold his share of both Gibson patents to a firm by the name of Crawley Metal Productions Ltd (CMR) whose Managing Director was a G.S. Blundell. As they too held the patent, this did not inhibit the Executive producing the machine in its own right or in partnership with anyone else. The 1945 Heads of Agreement with Gibson made it a condition that whosoever Gibson assigned his rights to under the patent, the Executive's interests remained protected. If the machine was to be developed commercially by outside interests, it might still benefit the Executive purchasing the machine by that means by invoking the clause limiting the price "to that not exceeding the prevailing price charged to other customers" less the royalty element. [13]

We have no insight into why this particular business, and not an established ticket machine manufacturer, purchased Gibson's share of the patent. CMR though had an important financial backer in the form of commercial banking and bullion giant N.M. Rothschild & Sons. This association also established a link with Royal Mint Refinery (RMR) Engineering Ltd of The Silk Mill, Brook Street, Tring, Middlesex, which was similarly owned by Rothschild and close to his country estate.

Set up as a shadow munitions factory during the Second World War, RMR Engineering had extensive workshops equipped with modern machine tools and a foundry, all obtained with the help of Ministry of Munitions subsidies. During the War, parts production for aero engines, aircraft airframes and tanks had been the norm but in peacetime the business was keen to diversify by attracting Government engineering contracts and making amongst other things, lipstick cases, successfully capturing the post-war market for cosmetics.

Crawley Metal Productions changed its name to Crawley Ticket Machines (CTM) in January 1950 with the clear intention of developing commercially the Gibson patent by utilising the financial backing of Rothschild and the manufacturing base at Tring. The Managing Director of this new enterprise, David Colville, wrote to the Executive in January 1950 saying his company was now the proprietor of the Gibson ticket machine and "should the Board decide to ask for quotations for the manufacture of this machine, we have no doubt that you will give us the opportunity of quoting".[14]

With the full scale trial with the pre-production machine only just beginning, Benford was obliged to decline Colville's offer of a meeting as there was as yet no basis to proceed with the offer. Colville wrote again in July, no doubt with some trepidation and clearly anxious to gather some insight into whether his company had purchased a winning design or potentially a 'lemon'. Under the pretext of Colville seeking insight in to any imperfections in the design to assist in the development of the new machine, fortuitously

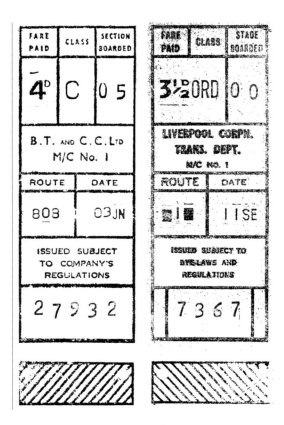

The answer to Colville's enquiry about the quantity required was settled by the Executive board of September 1950. Having approved the Gibson for large scale use, the agreed approach was somewhat cautious with approval for a batch of 2000 only, well short of the estimated total of 21,000 identified as needed to cover all road services. Significantly too, it authorised negotiations to begin with Crawley Ticket Machines, but the award of any contract would have to be by competitive tender. It was recognised that, while the Executive was free of course to acquire the machines it wanted from anywhere, the only company entitled to manufacture it, because it held the patent, was Crawley Ticket Machines.

Any thought of the Executive manufacturing the machine itself for its own requirements was dismissed at an early stage when it became clear that the Stockwell Punch Works lacked the additional 5000 square feet of floor space and facilities for 50 extra staff considered necessary to accomplish the task. Effra Road was considerably larger but still fully engaged with punch tickets. No doubt the recent debacle with the costs overrun for the pre-production machines was fresh in the mind too. It was recognised bulk orders from component suppliers, and the use of 'lower grade labour' that an outside supplier would invariably engage, delivered greater economies of scale than manufacture just for use in the Capital.

The necessary Special Expenditure Requisition (SER 21/2017) to purchase 2000 14-fare value Gibson machines, was authorised in October 1950 at an estimate of £27/0/0 per machine plus an additional 16/- for the fibre carrying box and 10/- per harness, the precise design of the latter now the focus of an Operational Research Team chaired by Dr A.W. Gilks, the Executive's Assistant Medical Officer.

his letter landed on the desk of David McKenna who, as Commercial Manager, now had overall responsibility for the service trial. As a result McKenna and Charles Speller duly met Colville and his co-directors on 28th July 1950.

Remarkably the notes from this meeting survive and the beginning of what turned out to be a very successful partnership was forged. A good rapport seems to have developed between McKenna and Colville, which helped considerably in the months ahead, ironing out the inevitable difficulties that would be faced getting the machine into production. Colville disclosed his company was in the process of building a number of prototypes and was starting to tool up for eventual production, therefore he needed to know the number of Gibsons the Executive required for tendering purposes. Insight too was being sought into operational experience with the pre-production batch and Speller assisted here as he had been largely responsible for building these machines. [15]

Left top: Gibson demonstrators circulated amongst bus operators in the 1950s—Bristol Tramways and Liverpool Corporation examples are shown here. Neither operator bought Gibsons in any quantity however; the Bristol company in common with other Tilling group members opted for the Setright SM.B while Liverpool was already a TIM and Ultimate user.
The adoption of a five digit ticket serial number for the Bristol example was very unusual and no doubt reflected the experience referred to in the text of the Gibson loaned to F.P. Arnold, of the Tilling Group Management Board, for use in Brighton.

This was a busy time for CTM preparing its manufacturing base at Tring and, pending the outcome of the London Transport tender, actively courting other customers for the new machine. Brochures were produced showing C.B.1 which was presumably on loan at the time, there being nothing more suitable to hand. The Gibson machine now has a name too, the 'A14', to emphasise its 14-fare value capability, no doubt to invite favourable comparison with the TIM12. Gibson demonstrators found their way to Sunderland, Bournemouth, Bristol Tramways, Birkenhead, Middlesbrough, Darwen and Eastbourne as well as, no doubt, those operators that were eventually equipped with the machine.[16]

Similarly, it wasn't unusual for requests for the loan of a machine to go direct to McKenna until CTM had sufficient demonstrators available. Middlesbrough Corporation requested a machine in September 1950 and a letter from F.P. Arnold in December 1950, who was Road Passenger Executive for the Tilling Group Management Board, asked for the loan of a machine for use by Brighton, Hove & District. A pre-production machine was loaned to Arnold for a weekend and it gave rise to some concern about the fare drum counters having only three digits. Brighton practice was for the ticket machine to 'follow the bus' and be used by several hands throughout the day. The number of low value tickets sold could exceed a thousand, giving a counter reading at the end of a shift appearing lower than at the start. This raised the prospect of the relative ease with which these counters could be 'clocked' (i.e. the machine rotated a sufficient number of times to bring the counter to a figure below the correct reading) thus inviting fraud. Modifying the fare drum to accommodate four-wheel counters was possible, but a simpler deterrent was simply adding an additional wheel to the 'total tickets' counter to record tens of thousands of revolutions thus making it impossible to disguise 'clocking' unless the machine was rotated considerably more times. In the event 'one machine per duty' practice in London limited, but never entirely eliminated, the opportunity for fraud and it was not considered a sufficient threat to make modifications to the total tickets counter. It has to be said though, the three-digit fare drum counter may well have deterred some potential Gibson customers like Brighton, Hove & District. In contrast, the adaptability of the TIM12 design to accommodate 4 or even 5 digit counters, clearly represented a safer option.

To gain access to the fare drum counters, 'blind head' security screws were fitted, one securing the end cap to the fare selector knob and another two to anchor the rectangular back plate. These are often mistaken for rivets, but are tapped to 6BA thread. On being tightened using a conventional screwdriver, the head was designed to break off leaving nothing behind that would allow the screw to be undone without cutting into it. Office staff were on the look out for any evidence of tampering with these screws which might indicate unauthorised access to the interior of the machine. As a precaution, fare drum counters were made to only increment upwards. At various times concerns were raised about attempts to interfere with the operation of the machine and one such occasion centred on Muswell Hill and Hemel Hempstead garages in 1967, to the extent that a revised end cap design was introduced for a pilot 100 machines utilising a lead seal. Quotations were sought from the manufacturer to supply 15,000 end caps of the revised design, but in the event this was not taken up.

Adolescence

In readiness for production, some detail changes were made to the design, partly to save costs but also in an effort to lighten it and preserve precious alloy. Most noticeable was a redesign of the curved fare drum cover which now assumed its familiar flat bottom appearance. A prototype production machine was demonstrated to the Central Bus Committee in November 1950 and it was noted the weight had been reduced from 4lb 3oz to only 3lb 15oz .[1]

Following on from this, tender invitations were sent out in December 1950 to close in mid January 1951, although this was subsequently extended to the end of the month. Three firms submitted tenders:

- Crawley Ticket Machines of Ifield Road, Crawley, with a sliding scale of prices from £27 per machine for 2000 to £24 per machine for an order of 10,000. Delivery was promised within 10 months of the date of the order (subject to metal availability) at a rate of 50 per week for the first 3 months, thereafter 100 per week.

- Clifford & Snell Ltd, a London based company established in 1929, and with a track record of pioneering electronic systems and devices, submitted a tender of £27/10/0 per machine for 2000 plus an additional £7000 for tooling. Delivery of a sample production machine was promised within 10 months from the date of the order and thereafter, at a reasonable rate (subject to materials availability).

Above: Taken from a contemporary Gibson brochure intended to attract the business of other bus operators, the choice of class of ticket codes aped London practice, although customers could specify what they wanted. No doubt the additional engraving costs so involved prompted some other UK customers to simply adopt London Transport practice.

The GIBSON A14
Portable Automatic
TICKET ISSUING MACHINE

SPECIFICATION

★ **USE.** For use by Transport undertakings, for issuing tickets on buses and trams.

★ **WEIGHT.** This does not exceed 4 lbs. including the ticket roll which issues 300 tickets.

★ **DIMENSIONS.** Height 7". Width 4½".

★ **METERS.** These register (i) the number of tickets sold in each value, (ii) the total number of tickets sold of all values.

★ **CONTROLS.** (A) Indicator wheel, which sets fares and revolves either way. (B) Fare stage number which is changed by a flick as the journey progresses. (C) Class of ticket control, which is changed to Ordinary, Return, Cheap-Day, Child, Midday, Transfer, and Workman's Return, with equal speed, having ordinary fare indicators in between other types. This control can also be turned either way. The machine can issue 14 different fare costs.

★ **TICKET ROLL.** This is plain paper and can be inserted in 15 seconds, but on issue the following is printed upon it : (I) date, (ii) number of ticket, (iii) fare stage, (iv) class of ticket, i.e. Ordinary, Return, Cheap-Day, Child, Midday, Transfer, and Workman's Return, (v) route number, (vi) cost of ticket, (vii) name of corporation or company issuing the ticket, (viii) No. of machine.

★ **SERVICEABILITY.** Great care was taken in the design to obviate wear on vital parts and the meter is so constructed that it cannot be tampered with.
The rustless hiduminium case is streamlined, and although light, is made to withstand hard usage.
All meters and controls are easily readable by the conductor whilst the machine is being worn.
Leather straps and backplates are supplied with the machine.
A compressed fibre case is also supplied in which to house the machine when not in use.

- P.A.M. Ltd, a now defunct concern, tendered a sliding scale of prices from £43/19/0 per machine for 2000 to £39/14/6 per machine for an order of 10,000. Tooling would be at an additional £3/3/0 to 7/6d per machine respectively (representing an overall tooling cost of £6216). Delivery would begin in November 1951 at 50 per month.

The CTM tender was the most attractive in terms of price and delivery, but the substantial discount for a quantity of 10,000 machines posed the question whether or not more than the authorised 2000 should be ordered. After some deliberation, and the need to get SER 21/2017 considerably revised upwards, the order was raised in April 1951 to CTM for 10,000 Gibson A14 machines at a total cost of £253,000 (£8 million in today's terms). Completion of the order was expected within 2 years 11 months and costs written off to revenue income and spread over 5 years.

A production planning meeting was convened in April 1951 and attended by McKenna, Speller and W. Hilton, the Executive's Purchasing Officer and for CTM, Colville and the RMR Engineering's Works Manager at Tring, J.L. Flynn. The need to reduce the reliance on die cast components, which were considered inferior in terms of strength and longevity, was discussed and Speller undertook to identify the components he wanted substituted. It was recognised this would adversely impact on cost by as much as 5/- for each machine. McKenna insisted that where subcontractors were used to produce components, no more than one firm should be involved for each item "to ensure absolute standardisation". Anyone having worked on Gibson machines for any length of time will appreciate that a very high degree of parts interchangeability was indeed achieved, greatly simplifying maintenance and repair. [2]

The initial hesitation over the size of the order may have been in part due to concerns over the likelihood of large scale redundancies in the back office staff involved in preparing the punch ticket boxes, occasioned by a rapid introduction of ticket machines that were far less labour intensive.

Above and right: More views of 'hybrid' pre-production Gibson no: 33, showing some of the features, such as the 'flat bottom' print drum cover, adopted for the production machine. It is likely that this was the machine demonstrated to the Central Bus Committee in November 1950. © TfL from the London Transport Museum collection

Opposite left: A Gibson stripped for overhaul by the author, all parts cleaned and ready for reassembly.

Opposite right: The first production machine, no 101, had this style of ticket but all subsequent machines, such as no 5551 shown here, placed the fare paid prominently at the top of the ticket.

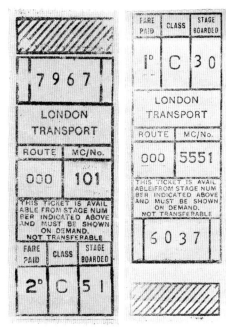

Materials shortages

It was not by chance that two of the three tenderers to manufacture the machine added caveats about metal availability. The first sign of problems ahead with the production process came in the form of a letter in April 1951 to RMR Engineering from the British Metal Corporation (BMC), their principal materials supplier, stating that they could not fulfil the order for aluminium alloy strip and rod needed to build many of the components. The Gibson specification required extensive use of a light, strong and easily workable aluminium alloy called 'hiduminium'. Supplied in a range of specifications for specific tasks, unfortunately this metal was also in heavy demand for the defence industry, at a time of increasing tension with the Soviet Union. It was extensively used for, amongst other strategic purposes, aircraft and missile production. Public transport operators were considered priority users but unfortunately there were insufficient material supplies to meet the burgeoning demand. In December 1950 it had been possible to sell the surplus Gibson parts to CTM left over from building the pre-production batch. Colville wrote to McKenna in April 1951 asking if there was anything he could

do to ease the shortage of metal "as I understand from Tring there is no official priority for anything and even aeroplane companies can get no special delivery". He goes on to say in the letter "the metal situation in the country seems to be getting increasingly bad and I am wondering whether you can approach the Ministry of Supply or Ministry of Transport with a view to strengthening BMC's case with T.I. Aluminium Ltd" (T.I. Aluminium was BMC's main supplier of smelted metal). [3]

The materials shortage was having a critical impact on the ability to produce the components necessary to build the machine and with UK suppliers unable to source sheet hiduminium, the search turned overseas. Colville received a telephone call from BMC on 17th May informing him that supplies were available from Germany. Hilton sent a memorandum to McKenna a few days later; "I would confirm in my experience of the present day supply position of aluminium alloy sheets that delivery is extremely protracted and in the circumstances, I should like to know if you consider it desirable that the obtaining of supplies from German sources should be pursued with the prospect of a further increase in price 2/3d per machine".

Sourcing aluminium alloy sheet abroad certainly helped ease the situation and by January 1952, the Tring factory was able to report it now had 25% of the 240 individual parts it lacked to build the machines, which it hoped to begin doing in April 1952. "The arms drive is making things very difficult as so many of our sub-contractors are asking for priority authorisation, especially for steel" wrote Colville. The Gibson machine has relatively little steel used in its construction, but one of the critical components made from it were the type plates which carry the characters that print the machine number, conditions of issue, title and fret on the tickets. These were produced from plain nickel steel sheet by a process known as 'electro forming'. Apparently RMR Engineering were 3½ tons short of the necessary steel plate to supply to their sub-contractor, Austin Miles Ltd, to make these. McKenna was able to offer 25 sheets of 14 gauge 126" by 37½" steel plate from Central Repair Depot Stores at Woolwich Road, Charlton which had been rendered surplus by tram abandonment. Unfortunately not all of this plate could be used as it had deep surface rusting. Flynn had the necessary steel for 7000 type plates by September 1952 but yet more steel had to be sourced from the Charlton stores to make up the shortfall.

McKenna was faced with a stark choice; swallow the increase in costs or risk delaying production of the machine another 6-12 months. I am sure too, a bitter sense of irony wasn't lost on those concerned. Barely 6 years earlier German Hiduminium had found its way to London in a far less constructive way in the form of V1 and V2 rockets.

Upper left: This ex-Douglas machine is in the process of being reassembled after the parts have been cleaned. The left hand side of the machine carries the print drum where the various type wheels necessary to produce the printed ticket are placed. The right hand side is given over to the print drum with its 14 counters for each fare value and the total tickets counter.

Left: The original engraved type wheel for printing the ticket serial number (one of a bank of 4) is shown (right) alongside the later wheel (left) produced by a rolling mill. The type is in shallow relief on the rolled wheel, and as such, was subject to wear far quicker. The engraved wheel is distinguishable on printed tickets by the absence of a serif on the '1' value, and as shown, the '4' facet had a characteristic flat top.

Opposite page: The earliest surviving 'long plate' machine is no 2295, which still carries the original thin type of fare selector and stage boarded knob. This style was apt to break and phased out from April 1954. Evident too from the photograph is the fare drum cover without the raised profile sections subsequently adopted to give the drum and total tickets counter greater internal clearance.

Design modifications

Mention has been made of London Transport's dislike of die casting and additional costs were incurred too by the requirement to perforate 12 individual internal components in an effort to save weight. The inking roller was redesigned and a more durable satinised aluminium fare strip adopted for the print drum.

The initial design for the type plate passed to CTM in July 1951 was identical to the one used for the pre-production batch. Very early machines produced by CTM would have printed tickets indistinguishable from the pre-production batch built at Stockwell (lending weight to the use or even re-use of early type plates touched on earlier). The opportunity was taken in October 1951 to redesign how the ticket was printed, and although the arbours carrying the type wheels inside the print drum were unaffected, by cleverly orientating the drum as a whole in relation to the start and stop point of each ticket issued, it was possible to put the fare, class and stage details at the top of the ticket and serial number at the bottom. Before, somewhat illogically, it had been the other way around.

In November 1950 the revised Gibson design was approved (with the 'flat bottom' fare drum casing) and with it other weight saving measures making it 4oz lighter. After the production line had been established, technical changes continued, often to generate savings in production costs and improve the life expectancy of components. These continued throughout the production run, less so in later years as operational experience of the Gibson grew. Most aren't readily noticeable but significant modifications did involve alterations to machines that had already entered service but usually put into effect when called in for overhaul.

Evidence of these changes is still apparent in some surviving Gibsons. Printing surfaces to the serial number and stage boarded type wheels were initially produced by being individually engraved, which was both time consuming and expensive, but from April 1954, these were produced far more cheaply by a rolling mill. Very occasionally machines still come to light that retain the original engraved style of type wheels. Control surfaces for changing the fares, class and stage boarded details were no longer produced in alloy but from a black machineable substance called ebonite, a sort of super-vulcanised rubber, or in moulded plastic. The biggest saving though was achieved by deleting the facility to print the date on tickets for all but a limited number of machines needed to equip routes in the Country Area, where return tickets were issued.

The downside of these changes was production delays and some confusion at Tring where, on occasions, pre-prepared tooling had to be scrapped. By March 1954, the modifications alone had increased the contract base price of £24 per machine to £24/15/8 with the dating facility as originally intended or £23/18/11 without it. This didn't include increased production, labour and raw materials costs. A 'rise and fall' mechanism was included in the contract with CTM (which had rebranded itself Ticket

Equipment Ltd or TEL in January 1952) to accommodate such fluctuations and overall it was agreed this should be settled by applying an extra 7½% to the cost of the first 2000 machines produced, a hike of £1/16/0 for each one, bringing the total to £25/16/0. From the 2001st machine onwards, the price would be £25/19/6.

These increases were not unexpected and reflected similar rises in costs throughout the Executive's operating base. Indeed E.C. Ottaway, the Chief Supplies Officer, commented "the contractor has been very reasonable, has produced an excellent machine at a low cost compared with similar models and has accepted considerable risks in undertaking what really amounted to a development contract". [4]

Deliveries of production machines begin

The shortage of raw materials and the large number of amendments (104 items by mid 1955) inevitably had a detrimental affect on the delivery schedule. The contract anticipated the first deliveries in February 1952, but by January 1953, other than a handful of test machines for quality control purposes, nothing had been received. Two production Gibsons were tested in service later that

month, one at Hendon and the other at Hanwell for trolleybus route 607. But there had been disappointment that the new 'state of the art' bus garage at Stockwell had to be equipped with punches when it opened in April 1952 and the same was true at Norbiton the following month.

The first batch of any quantity were the 60 machines received in April 1953 and earmarked for use at Isleworth for route 657 where they entered service the following month, the serviceability of the last TIM9s by then at breaking point. As was seen with the influx of TIM12s, ironically this meant machines replacing other machines again when the principal purpose was to mechanise and eliminate punch tickets from everyday use.

By the Spring of 1953, capacity at Tring to produce the Gibson at the 50 per month promised was still well below par prompting Colville to write to McKenna "we are determined to stand on our own feet and give you the production you ask for, but you have said in the past that you would prefer a small rate to begin with rather than wild promises which cannot be fulfilled".

Evidently staffing problems at Tring were now adding to the log jam. A youthful George Sawyer, a later Ticket Machine Works Manager, was despatched to the factory to help out and by the end of April 1953, a further 217 machines were ready for delivery and a rate of 15 completions a day was being achieved. Colville wrote "it is no good disguising the fact however, that this target has only been achieved as a result of the great help given to us by your Mr Sawyer. The final touches to the machine, which require an experienced instrument maker, have proved a much worse bottleneck

Above: Another very rare surviving long plate Gibson — in this case no 5886 and carrying 'A' and 'B' letter codes for early morning single tickets. The 'B' category was not used after December 1955. This machine was the subject of the publicity photograph reproduced on the inside of the front cover.

than Flynn ever anticipated. Our own man can manage from 6 to 7 machines a day only and Sawyer has been doing 8 or 9". [5]

In response to the need for commitment on the rate of Gibson delivery from Ticket Equipment Ltd, Colville wrote '"you may think this totally inadequate and rather a foolish answer to your demand for a firm, detailed programme, but I cannot quite see how I can improve on it at the moment. Of course we could keep Sawyer…".

Unfortunately George Sawyer was urgently needed back with his employer, but his association with the Gibson was to last throughout his long period of service with London Transport and beyond.

There were a few teething problems not unexpectedly with the new machines for Isleworth; the ticket crumpling problem hadn't gone away evidently although mostly due to tickets being incorrectly torn off at issue. There were some instances too of stiffness in operation and the main screw holding the end cap to the fare selector knob tended to loosen allowing it to fall off. This latter fault was corrected by fitting a modified end cap fixing.

Fulwell was the next depot to receive Gibsons in August 1953 and some criticism of the new machines appeared in the following week's 'Surrey Comet'. The article claimed conductors at Fulwell found the machine "much slower" than the old TIM machines they have been used to for years and apparently resented having to turn the fare knob repeatedly rather than simply 'dialling up' the required fare. Sensitivities were aroused and the Executive's Chairman, John Elliott, asked for a report on the matter, but the complaints quickly melted away as the machine became established and staff became used to it.

The punch conversion programme

A strategy meeting was convened in August 1952 involving all relevant tier 2 operational managers to devise a Gibson implementation programme.[6] Overall it had to be route focused and meet these key objectives:

- Priority to garages and depots still using TIM9 machines to allow these to be withdrawn;
- Avoidance of 'mixed ticketing' arrangements by wholesale conversion of garages and depots to Gibson, and ideally where routes are shared between garages, conversion of all simultaneously;
- Balanced apportionment between operating districts to avoid "excessive female staff redundancies"

- 10% of new machines to be allocated to Country garages in response to concerns expressed earlier by B.H. Harbour, the Country Buses and Coaches Operating Manager, that Central Road Services would receive a disproportionate allocation;
- Priority to Country garages operating Green Line coach routes (which will be using Setright machines) where weekend augmentation of such services by drafting in buses from other garages, would otherwise involve a mix of punch and machine ticket issues for the same route.

The requirement to avoid 'mixed ticketing' arrangements per route, garage or depot were not wholly achieved and particularly in the Country area there are documented instances of punch and machine produced tickets, more commonly Setright issues, rubbing shoulders with punch tickets as late as 1957.

The proposed conversion programme and actual changeover date (where known) is set out in Appendix 1. Tracking the various garage and depot conversions is difficult to say the least and this is evident from the large number of subsequent redrafts of the original programme devised in March 1954. Mostly this was due to the unpredictable rate that machines left the factory, although by mid 1954 this was being sustained at the rate of 100 per week as promised in the original tender.

After Fulwell, there was then a hiatus to allow production to build up with Southall the next conversion in November 1953 and the first garage where Gibsons replaced punch tickets, closely followed by Hanwell two weeks later. Garston was the first Country Area garage to migrate to the new machine, all by the close of 1953.

Conversions then continued at the rate of one or two garages per month until the pace picked up in June 1954, thereafter usually 3 garages or depots per month were converted. In all, by the end of September 1954, 22 Central Road Services garages and depots had been converted accounting for 3930 machines in service and the Country Area accounted for a further 7 garages and 447 machines. With the exception of Northfleet, all the Country conversions by this date were concentrated in the North West operating area. Grouping garages in this way made the inevitable teething problems more manageable given the travel distances for the centrally based staff involved.

By August 1955, 50 garages and depots in the Central Area had been equipped with Gibsons and 12 in the

Left: The name of George Sawyer first enters the official record in April 1953 when he was despatched to Tring to assist Crawley Ticket Machines on the newly established assembly line. He is pictured here, seated right, in February 1955 with Craftsman John Stephens at the Stockwell Punch works, getting newly delivered machines ready for service. © TfL from the London Transport Museum collection

Country Area; 9666 machines had been issued for these conversions with a further 7998 needed for the remainder (17,664 in total). The Executive Conference of May 1954 had authorised a second order of 7000 machines from TEL at a price of £26/5/0 each. These were numbered from 10101 onwards. [7]

The conversion programme was intended to conclude by the end of 1956, but it continued throughout 1957 with the last new machines, in fulfilment of the second order for 7000, received from TEL at the end of October 1957. The last Central Area garages to change over were Battersea, Merton, Sutton and in the Country Area, Crawley, Dorking and Reigate were all converted by the end of 1957.

Some controversy exists over which garage or depot had the distinction of being the very last to use punch tickets (regardless of when they received Gibson machines). While there is no official record to support this, one source credits West Ham and Poplar as being the last to use punches for anything other than emergency use and football specials, on 5th October 1958. If this date is correct, this would have been more than five years after the Isleworth conversion and nearly 13 years after Gibson machines had first been used in service, albeit experimentally. It had

indeed been a rather long and winding road to achieve full mechanisation.

As a final footnote to this chapter, there was still the matter of the TIM12 machines to address which, although still relatively modern, were now non-standard, so it was decided to replace these too with Gibsons. Of the 1000 TIM12s purchased, only 660 remained in use in April 1957 and maintenance was becoming increasingly expensive. The conversion progamme published in 1956 proposed Victoria the first to go on 9th August 1959 (139 machines), followed by Camberwell the following Sunday (226 machines) and concluding with Cricklewood on August 21st (251 machines). In the event it was Camberwell that hung on their TIMs longest, the actual conversion date being 27th September 1959.

Tellingly the last TIM conversions were achieved by using Gibsons from the 17,000 previously purchased but no longer needed to cover what was by now a steadily falling number of duties. London Transport was no exception to a decline in bus route mileage brought about by increased car ownership throughout the 'fifties and the appearance of more televisions in people's homes meaning fewer evening trips out to the cinema.

No new Gibson machines had entered London service for five years prior to the end of London's trolleybuses on 8th May 1962 when this famous publicity still was taken. The photographer was anxious to capture both conductor with his trusty Gibson and driver, perhaps contemplating retirement as well. Not so the Gibson machine, which had only just begun its career with another three decades of use ahead. © TfL from the London Transport Museum collection

Maturity

The design changes that had hampered getting the machine into production didn't end when the last machines were delivered from TEL. A series of further significant changes to the specification and modifications were necessary to keep the machine fit for purpose throughout its long working life.

Fare range

One of the weaknesses of the Gibson, indeed any machine with a fixed range of fare values, is the need for internal modification when the fare values it was built with cease to apply. This was recognised from the outset by those such as Benford and McKenna who considered it a price worth paying to obtain the valuable statistical information only possible with a machine able to record ticket sales of every fare value. The need for ongoing modification to take account of fares increases was seen as manageable, given the relatively low inflation economy of the 1950s and 1960s and a maximum life expectancy of the machine of 15 years.

As originally ordered, the batch of 10,000 Central Area Gibsons had a fare range of 1d, 2d, 2½d, 3d, 3½d, 4d, 5d, 6d, 7d, 8½d, 9d, 10d, 1/- and 2/-. This range was not ideally matched to the new fare scale introduced in 1954 and

Right: Fare strips from Gibson machines during the pre-decimal era, (1) very early production machines had this scale until 1954; (2) the 'Universal Fare Band' introduced in December 1955 with the 'A' value for Early Morning Single issues; (3) the revised scale from 1964 with higher values and no EMS code and (4) the Country 'Range B' scale from 1962 which allowed for the issue of Green Rover tickets.

Next page: Taken from an official document showing the proposed 'short plate' ticket layout—15001 (right) would have been the first machine produced but the new sequence was begun instead at 20001 to allow a sufficiently big gap with the last long plate machines. Notable too is the Country Area long plate machine equipped with a type wheel for the issue of return tickets, produced in limited numbers after April 1954 and (centre) the final long plate layout for the Central Area with the 'wide' fare type wheel and missing section of fret, introduced in January 1955.

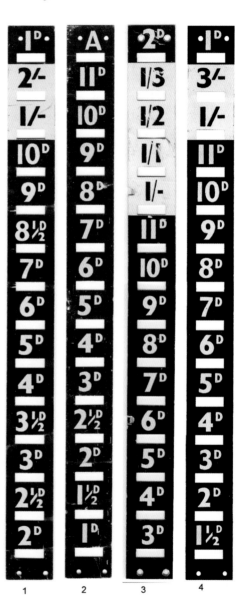

1   2   3   4

machines still under construction, and built subsequently, were delivered with a revised fare scale of A, B, 1d, 1½d, 2d, 2½d, 3d, 4d, 5d, 6d, 7d, 9d, 11d, and 1/-. The 'A' and 'B' values were to enable two different 'Early Morning Single' (EMS) fares, 4d and 5d respectively, to be recorded separately from other fares. The 'EMS' category had been introduced in 1950 on withdrawal of workmen's return fares (one of the obstacles to mechanisation of ticket issue) and was available for travel from 3:00am weekdays providing the destination was reached by 8:00am. At different times, the codes represented different EMS fares, for example in 1955 'A' was equivalent to a 7d fare and 'B' thereafter was not used. In 1957 'A' meant a 9d EMS issue and in 1959, a 1/- EMS ticket. The 'EMS' code on the class wheel was not to be used after 1955 as the letter code was sufficient recognition with the fare drum counter providing the necessary statistical information.

Piecemeal changes to machines' fare range then gave rise to the logistical complexity of Gibsons with two different fare ranges being in use at the same time, made worse by a further revision to fares in June 1955, with the effect that the fare range needed to alter again to A, B, 1d, 1½d, 2d, 2½d, 3d, 4d, 5d, 6d, 7d, 8d, 10d and 1/-.

While it was feasible to convert machines with an earlier fare range to the current one at overhaul, it was estimated that changing the fare wheels for all 17,000 machines simultaneously would take between 18 months and 2 years. This meant the rate of upgrading machines to the current scale was being outstripped by changes to the fare scales themselves. This in time meant machines with three different fare ranges came to be in use at the same time. This proved highly confusing for all concerned, compounded by differing rules in the correct issue of 'EMS' and combination tickets depending on the fare scale of the machine in use.

Fares changed again in December 1955, and a new Gibson fare range accordingly; A, 1d, 1½d, 2d, 2½d, 3d, 4d, 5d, 6d, 7d, 8d, 9d, 10d and 11d. At this point an attempt was made to establish these values as the 'Universal Fare Band' to halt the merry-go-round of continually replacing fare print wheels. Covering all intermediate fare values to 11d, this effectively held the line until 1964 when fares inflation required a revised range of 2d, 3d, 4d, 5d, 6d, 7d, 8d, 9d, 10d, 11d, 1/-, 1/1d, 1/2d and 1/3d to be introduced. With the ending of EMS issues, the 'A' value was no longer required. It was in this latter form that Central Area Gibsons remained in use until the introduction of decimal currency in 1971.

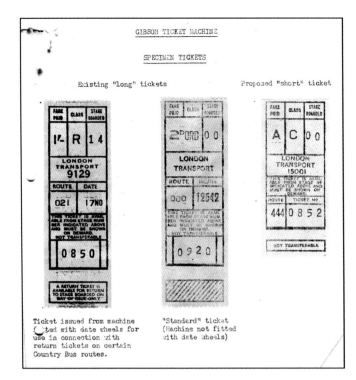

GIBSON TICKET MACHINES

SPECIMEN TICKETS

Existing "long" tickets — Proposed "short" ticket

Ticket issued from machine fitted with date wheels for use in connection with return tickets on certain Country Bus routes.

"Standard" ticket (Machine not fitted with date wheels)

Turning to the Country Area machines, the same pressures applied, if anything made worse by longer routes and higher fares and the complication of accommodating other operator's fares structures for joint workings. Fare revisions in December 1955 and September 1957 indicate three different fare ranges in use. The Central Area 'Universal Fare Band' of 1955 was applied to Country scales from November 1959 and remained in step until 1962 when the fare print wheels had to be altered to accommodate the mechanisation of issuing Green Rover tickets featuring a 3/- fare and a 1/- fare (in combination with 6d) for child issues. The need for ½d fares no longer applied to all garages; the opportunity was therefore taken to include more higher fare values in the Gibson scale where ½d fares did not apply. This became 'Range A'; 2d, 3d, 4d, 5d, 6d, 7d, 8d, 9d, 10d, 11d, 1/-, 1/1d, 1/2d and 3/-. 'Range B' included the ½d fare in keeping with but not identical to the 'Universal Fare Band' of 1d, 1½d, 2d, 3d, 4d, 5d, 6d, 7d, 8d, 9d, 10d, 11d, 1/- and 3/-. Range 'C' simply referred to Central Area machines with the 1955 'Universal Fare Band'.

49

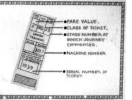

FARE PAID	CLASS	STAGE BOARDED
1'-	ORD	1 0

LONDON TRANSPORT
25015

THIS TICKET IS AVAILABLE FROM STAGE Nº INDICATED ABOVE AND MUST BE SHOWN ON DEMAND.

ROUTE	TICKET Nº
201	0 2 3 5

NOT TRANSFERABLE

The garages with 'Range A' machines at that time were Dartford, Epping, Garston, Grays, Hatfield, Hertford, Leatherhead, Luton and Swanley. 'Range B' garages were Addlestone, Amersham, Chelsham, Crawley, Dorking, Dunton Green, East Grinstead, Godstone, Guildford, Hemel Hempstead, High Wycombe, Northfleet, Reigate, St Albans, Staines, Stevenage, Tring and Windsor.

The typeface used on the fare wheels changed little throughout the production run, but a wider style was devised in January 1955, requiring removal of the dividing fret between the fare and class value. The purpose is unclear, but may have been an effort to make the fare value on the ticket more prominent, perhaps to deter the fraudulent practice of issuing a ticket of a lower value than the fare paid. This modification was for long associated with Alperton garage (which had been converted to Gibsons in late 1953) and many in use there were of this type. Introduction of the 'wide value' fare print wheel took place in the middle of the production run of the second batch of machines and typically those supplied new with this feature are in a 12xxx or 13xxx numbering sequence. Some earlier machines with lower numbers were converted too to the wider fare wheel at overhaul. It is not unusual therefore to find tickets from 10xxx and 11xxx series machines with the wide fare wheel; the lowest numbered machine discovered yet is 1793.

After the 'long plate' format was abandoned, the wider fare wheel style fell out of favour, possibly for aesthetic reasons. Indeed it is rare to find tickets of this type, as it was largely confined to issues in 1955 and 1956 only. The wide type wheel and the 'long' style of type plate itself would both be swept away in subsequent modifications.

Top: Concerns were raised that Gibson tickets, unlike the punch equivalents they replaced, were not readily recognisable to passengers in respect of the fare they had paid, which opened the door to the possibility of fraud. In response, a 'know your ticket' publicity campaign was launched with in-vehicle advertising.

Above: A pristine surviving short plate Gibson and ticket—the machine number, 25015, was carried on a tag attached to the front cover which covered up the engraved number it had hitherto carried in long plate guise.

Right: Debate continued until almost the end of Gibson operation as to whether or not Central Area machines should be capable of issuing Rover tickets in anticipation of a decision to allow 'on the bus' sales. Although this practice was adopted in the Country Area in 1962, due to concerns over lost revenue from hard pressed conductors distracted from the task of day-to-day fare collection, Red Rovers continued to be only available from approved vendors such as Underground stations and Central Area bus garages.

Redesign of the type plate

Until half way through the second batch of 7000 Gibsons, machines were manufactured with the 'long' type of type plate producing a ticket of approximately 4" in length (10.25cm) as per the original design. It wasn't an efficient use of ticket roll paper though, as sections of the ticket were left blank, for example the 'hatched out' bottom panel that contained conditions of issue for return tickets in the case of the relatively few machines needing this facility. Reducing the length of the ticket to approximately 3ins (7.75cm) would mean a drop in ticket roll consumption of 20% with another 30 tickets possible per roll, or put simply, a saving at 1956 prices of £22,000 per annum and an extra 30 tickets per roll. [1]

Flynn proposed merely substituting a shorter plate by removing the bottom ½" but making no other changes and 60 machines of this type were apparently trialled at Isleworth. Speller came up with an alternative 'short plate' solution, which was the one that was adopted, which involved repositioning the route number as it appeared on the printed ticket next to the serial number, which no longer sat in the middle, but shifted to one side. Unfortunately repositioning the type wheels meant internal alterations to the print drum and to the shutter on the front cover of the machine to allow access to the repositioned route type wheels, so they could still be reset. All of the first 10,000 machines from the first batch, and those already delivered or complete awaiting delivery to long plate format from the

second, would need to be returned to TEL or retained for the conversion work to be done. The agreed cost was £4/14/3 per machine, of which £2/0/3 would be just for the new type plate and carrier assembly. Consideration was given to the Ticket Machine Works undertaking the conversion work, but routine servicing and upgrading machines to the latest fare scale had to take priority, and they lacked spare capacity to do the work.

Short plate conversions began in late 1955 and were completed by the end of 1956. The overall cost was £201,147 but this includes a number of other modifications to improve reliability in the light of operational experience with the Gibson and the cost of new fare wheels to keep track of fares increases. [2] The short plate conversion alone would have cost approximately £60,000 of this total which, if the ticket roll savings predicted are to be believed, would have been recouped within 3 years.

In all, approximately 14,000 machines were converted with the final 3,000 deliveries of the second batch of 7000 escaping modification and built to short plate specification from new. A long plate Gibson carrying machine no 13956 is representative of the boundary between the last new long-ticket machines and replacement on the production line with those with the short plate. No records exist to determine the exact changeover point but the original intention to begin the short plate sequence at machine no 15001 was later revised upwards to begin instead at no 20001 to avoid any risk of an overlap.

The old long plate identity of renumbered machines was concealed by fitting a small metal tag bearing the new machine number to the front cover, although the interchangeability of parts as machines were serviced (rather like London Transport's bus overhaul system) meant that the old number on a machine doesn't reliably indicate it's original identity. Assuming all 17,000 Gibsons of both batches received short plates, then we can estimate the highest numbered machines in the short plate numbering sequence were in a 36xxx series though of course much higher numbered machines are still extant, up to 38xxx in fact, which is accounted for by the replacement of worn-out type plates. There was never any attempt to replace the plate with one that kept the original machine number: this was simply discarded and a new type plate and identity allocated.

Before leaving the subject of type plates, these were always made of steel to ensure the printing face remained

printing surface. Unfortunately the plates so produced were not as hardwearing as hoped for and showed significant wear after only 250,000 tickets; the experiment was therefore discontinued in July 1964. A total of 500 replacement steel plates had to be ordered from TEL in December that year at a cost of £3/5/2 each (£60 in today's terms).

As related below, this wasn't quite the end of the long plate machines which lingered for longer in the Country Area.

Rover tickets
Freedom tickets were introduced to the Country Area in two stages—for the Southern Division from May 1956 and in the Northern Division in July 1956. The 'Green Rover' as it was known, was available for unrestricted travel after 9:30am weekdays and Saturdays and all day Sundays and Bank Holidays. From July 1961 rover tickets were available all day Saturdays. The Red Rover, the Central Area equivalent, was introduced the following year. Both were priced at 5/- (the equivalent of £6 today) for an adult or 2/6d for a child. They proved popular from the outset – 271,177 Green Rovers were sold in the 12 months ending 5th October 1957 and 164,985 Red Rovers for the equivalent period a year later. Green Rovers were sold on the bus by the validation of a pre-printed ticket with the conductor clipping the appropriate day and month with hand nippers. Tickets were colour co-ordinated with various overprints to ensure that the ticket could not be reused. The congestion on Central buses meant it was only practical to offer them through Underground stations, some mainline BR railway stations, the 490 London Coastal Coaches street front agents and a further 722 retail outlets.[3]

legible over millions of ticket issues. After 8 years' use, however, these were becoming worn and replacements in metal were expensive to produce. An experiment was therefore conducted to produce type plates using a photo polymer material that hardened on contact with ultraviolet light. The parts of the plate in relief were shielded from the light source and these could be later dissolved, leaving the hardened material upstanding to form the

Above: A delightful view of staff posing against an H1 class trolleybus—the youthful, idealistic conductor and his driver, contemplating what one can wistfully imagine upwards of 40 years service driving trolleybuses, and trams no doubt before that. In reality the number of the driver's Metropolitan Stage Carriage badge would indicate a post War issue. © TfL from the London Transport Museum collection

Right: The Gibson was not ideally suited to one person operation but nevertheless they were used in that way on the Country Area's diminutive GS class. GS 15 is pictured here and owned by Mick Speller, the grandson of Charles Speller. The ticket illustrated is a Country Area Gibson issue with the characteristic dating facility.

It was not thought practical for a Gibson machine to handle such high value cash transactions without modification to include 2/6d and 5/- fare values which would effectively reduce the fare range of the machine for day-to-day fare collection purposes to just 12 values. Moreover, the dating facility had been deleted early in Gibson production to save costs and hitherto, no machines to short plate specification had this facility. In those few instances where return tickets had to be issued that required a dating function, all in the Country Area, a handful of Gibsons had been built with this capability in 1954. All were to long plate layout and remained a feature of Gibson operations at Epping and later Harlow, and not finally retired until 10th March 1967, long after their Central Area cousins had become extinct.

While misgivings remained about sale of Red Rovers using Gibsons on inner London routes, the

speed and convenience of being able to do so gave rise to the decision in June 1962 to modify the fare range of Country Gibsons to allow this. A 3/- value was therefore included in the fare range of Country machines, which corresponded to the cost at the time of a child Green Rover and half the cost of an adult one (which could be handled by a double issue).

The three route number type wheels were removed, two being reused for the date and the third replaced by a new month type wheel which was slightly wider, so minor modification was necessary to the type plate and its carrier. The obsolete 'route' reference on the type plate was simply ground off – new type plates were not fitted, so the word 'date' was never printed on the ticket, merely a blank space. The altered type plate, the existence of a dating facility and a 3/- fare value are the principal means of identifying Gibsons used in the Country Area.

Unfortunately no records exist confirming the exact number of Country machines so converted, but a reasonable estimate is in the region of 1600. Garston was the first garage to get them, in December 1962, working garage by garage through all 27 ending at Northfleet in February 1963. From July 1963, the

unused class value C/M served to designate child Green Rover tickets but this practice had ceased by 1966 when 'C' was used – the equivalent adult ticket again used 'COM' in keeping with normal practice for handling combination issues.

As the Gibson dating facility was unable to designate the year of issue, Country Area ticket rolls were colour co-ordinated depending on the year in question. Starting in 1963 with yellow ticket rolls, pink rolls were used in 1964 and green ones the following year. This of course would be for all tickets issued, not just Rovers. The sequence repeated again in 1966 with yellow and continued in this way until 1971, thereafter plain white paper rolls were used. After the demise of the Country Gibsons in mid 1974, Rover tickets were produced by the replacement Almex A machines which had the added advantage they could print the year of issue.

Above: Gibson class and pre-decimal fare type wheels were engraved individually; a costly and laborious process in the days before CNC production processing. The stage number type wheels are of the type produced by a roll mill.

Right page: The wooden cradle used in traffic offices to support the machine for the benefit of clerical staff. (Photograph courtesy of Andrew Jeffreys).

The ability to produce Green Rover tickets by deletion of the route details as printed on the ticket decided the eventual fate of the 1200 remaining Country Gibsons. After withdrawal, they were sold back to London Transport in August 1975. Unsuitable for further service use, their value lay only as a source of salvageable spare parts. [4]

One person operation

When the Gibson was designed, its primary purpose was for use by a roving conductor and carried about the person on a suitable harness. Very little thought was giving to adaptability to a static application. This issue presented itself early on as a suitable means needed to be provided to adequately support the machine for the benefit of traffic office staff preparing Gibsons for service and cross-referencing counter readings at duty end. A rather crude wooden cradle was devised for the purpose but this wasn't adequate anchorage to enable tickets to be issued or secure the machine to a moving vehicle.

The need for a suitable ticket machine for a new generation of rural buses intended for one person operation arose in 1953. With only 26 seats and with special legal dispensation to be operated without a conductor, the GS class was intended for Country Buses routes serving narrow lanes and sparsely populated areas. In such an environment, full size vehicles would have been difficult to operate and takings scarcely justified the wages of two people. Initially drivers were equipped with ticket punches and a rack. As Country garages operating GS buses came to be converted to Gibson machines, thought had to be given to how its compact but somewhat irregular shape could be held securely in reach of the driver.

The answer came in the form of an ergonomically designed cradle with an arm that fastened over the ticket spool cover, securing the machine to the cab bulkhead. It could be moved into position for collecting fares and then pushed back into a wooden housing when not in use on a short section of track. This wooden housing even had a lockable lid so the machine could be left safely if the vehicle was unattended. In spite of the narrow confines of the GS cab, this arrangement worked relatively satisfactorily but it was not thought feasible to scale this up for more busy routes. With the use of RF class buses for one person operation later in the 1950s, the Ultimate was considered a more suitable candidate and it was this machine, not the Gibson, that was adopted for the role.

Despite the difficulty of securing the Gibson to a bulkhead for one person operation, an experiment using 29 machines on full-size buses was conducted as late as October 1968 on route 251 operating from Edgware garage using RF buses. The buses had already been in use in that capacity with experimental Almex A.763 (magnetic tape) machines. The reason for using Gibsons may be linked to the late delivery and subsequent unreliability of a new experimental machine, the Setright SM.D, that would have furthered one person operation by the release of Ultimate machines from the Country Area for their use in the Capital. As explored in a subsequent chapter, the failure of this experiment may have prompted London Transport to turn to old ideas, although the use of Gibsons in this role does smack a little of desperation. At the time, route 251 was designated something of a guinea pig for 'driver only' experiments. Although it was doubtful there was ever any serious expectation that the Gibson was suited to that purpose, nevertheless it was necessary to put the matter to the test in preparation for large scale migration to one person operation for inner London routes, a role that the Ultimate, and later the Almex E machine, was far more capable of fulfilling. It is likely the Gibson cradles developed for the GS were used, no doubt recycled given by that stage the fleet of these little Guy buses was becoming depleted.

Ultimate machines replaced the Gibsons for one person workings at Edgware in January 1969 and the results analysed. Ticket issue was between 1 and 1.9 seconds slower compared to the Almex and the awkward rotational movement required (rather than the back and forward motion of the Almex) meant more that one hand was needed. Of the 30 drivers engaged on route 251, 28 considered the Gibson inferior and the age-old problem of tickets crumpling and jamming inside the machine reappeared, due to passengers snatching tickets from the machine, rather than waiting to be handed them by the driver. To keep the momentum going, a further 248 Ultimate machines were ordered from Bell Punch in May 1969 as a stop-gap to progress one person operation; by then the prospect was rapidly receding of sufficient Setright SM.Ds ever being received from the manufacturer in time.

Driver use of Gibson machines ended in March 1972 with the withdrawal of the last GS class vehicle but it is worth mentioning that it did, however, find a successful 'one person operation' role for itself with the largest user outside London, the Melbourne & Metropolitan Tramways Board in Australia.

Before we leave the 1960s, that decade icon the AEC/PRV Routemaster, London's standard double deck bus of the era, has an association in many people's minds with the Gibson. This is perhaps because both are commonly portrayed together, having in common a standardised design eminently fitted for the intended purpose and a degree of 'over engineering' that allowed service lives considerably longer than envisaged when they entered service. It conjures up memories for many of mini-skirts, cars with fins and rock n'roll!

Into the 1970s - decimal currency

As early as 1966, the Ticket Machine Works, which had migrated to Effra Road, Brixton in the previous decade, was considering the impact of Britain abandoning its age-old monetary system of shillings and pence and adopting decimal currency instead. The move was duly approved by the Government that year with the intended implementation date of 15th February 1971. London Transport planned to convert one day early on Sunday February 14th preferring to use a quieter travelling day to help bed in the changes. The Underground system duly converted on that day but it was decided to defer the change for bus operations until the following Sunday, 21st February 1971 to allow the new coinage to circulate. Sunday conversions reflected well established practice; garage by garage changeovers to Gibsons had invariably taken place on a Sunday.

'D Day', as it affectionately came to be known, would see dual use of currency for a period while the old '£.s.d.' coins were phased out. Only the old sixpence coin or 'tanner', the shilling (5p) and the florin (10p) would continue as legal tender beyond the initial transitional period. Henceforth £1 would be made up of 100 'p' not the 240 pennies of old. New ½p, 1p and 2p coins appeared and the old 'half crown' 2/6d coin had been phased out in 1970, so too the 10/- note in favour of a new 50p coin.

There was some debate whether or not ½p values needed to be included in London's new decimal currency fare scale, as the old ½d had disappeared from fare ranges in 1959, when children's half fares were rounded up to the nearest penny. The concern was that as a public body, London Transport wasn't seen to be profiteering by rounding up fares on translation to their decimal equivalent. The decision had been taken by the Government in April 1970 to retain the old 6d coin for only a period of 3 years after 'D Day'. The

Above: Conductor Mrs M Sherlock of New Cross garage pictured in December 1965 with her Gibson. Note the use of a leather backing apron to protect the tunic from abrasion and the tunic's patch pockets, possibly to discourage their use for loose change in favour of the cash bag. © TfL from the London Transport Museum collection

Right page: Decimalisation presented challenges to London Transport as all remaining Gibson machines in service had to have a new decimal currency fare type wheel fitted. Although these were produced quickly and cheaply by the rolling process (as were the later alpha wheels), it wasn't possible to convert all the machines needed by 'D Day'. As a stop gap, the 'split fare' strip was introduced showing both old currency values and their decimal equivalent side by side. The 'd' value was simply ground off the fare type wheel which could be done without the need to strip the machine down. Illustrated are (left to right), the Central Area 'split' fare strip; an equivalent Country Area strip and the strip fitted to fully decimalised machines. With usage of Gibson machines not expected to last more than a couple of years at most, Country Area 'decimal ready' machines were never fully converted and retained the 'split' value strip to the end. The tickets illustrated are Country Area (upper) and Central Area decimal issues.

6d pre-decimal fare directly related to the 2½p face value of the old 'tanner'. Similarly the old '3d bit' would equate to a 1½p fare, 1/6d to 7½p and 2/6d to 12½p. To preserve strict equivalence with the old and new currency values, the Gibson decimal range adopted therefore consisted of 1½p, 2p, 2½p, 3p, 4p, 5p, 6p, 7p, 7½p, 8p, 9p, 10p, 11p, and 12½p. Adopting ½p values in many respects was a backward step by 'cluttering up' the fare range which could have been made coarser by inclusion of a wider range of values to make it more 'future proof'.

New decimal value fare wheels and strips for the fare drum were ordered in September 1970, the former of the rolled type and produced by English Numerical Machines Ltd. Before doing so, consideration was given to a 'coded' system whereby the old pence value printed on the ticket corresponded to a decimal currency fare (the 'd' being filed off) and values 1/- and over could be used as a code for an unrelated decimal fare over 11p. Codes to represent fare values would get round the need to keep changing the type wheels with each fare rise. It had been dismissed principally by the Traffic Auditor who had been concerned that as Gibson tickets represented 90% of the total sold, there could be a large loss of revenue from 'overriding' and fraud where tickets had no apparent face value. [5]

This all meant, of course, another round of internal modifications to the machine to fit new decimal type wheels and fare strips. In the case of the oldest machines, this was the fourth or fifth such change. There would also be the need to reprint waybills and the ready reckoner used to work out cash receipts from fare drum counter readings. The estimated cost of all this for the Central Area would be £22,500, of which £10,000 would be for materials to convert the minimum of 8200 machines estimated as required for duty purposes on 'D Day'. An additional 2015 machines were needed as spares and a float for servicing purposes while a further 2600 unserviceable machines languished at Effra Road, some of which could readily be made useable. As the priority was to ensure as many as possible fully decimalised machines were ready for use on the due date, a pool was built up from spare Gibsons not immediately required for service. For the remainder, a Central Area dual fare strip was fitted to all machines that couldn't be fully decimalised in time. This enabled both the old currency fare, and its decimal equivalent alongside, to be displayed in the machine's fare drum viewing window.

By this time London Transport's Country Buses and Coaches department had gone its own way, having passed to the newly formed National Bus Company in 1969. For the 900 Country Gibsons estimated to be still needed for use in February 1971 (all 'A' range), a different solution was decided upon reflecting the far more limited life expectancy of the machine due to the wholesale planned introduction of one person operation. The dual fare strip solution was adopted as a permanent means of decimalising machines needed for service and the fare wheel amended by simply grinding off the 'd' against the relevant fare value – 3d therefore became '3' - the 'p' wasn't printed on the ticket. Shillings values were unaffected and as with the Central Area, these functioned as the equivalent for the new decimal value – i.e. 3/- became 15p. London Country machines still printed 'London Transport' on tickets in spite of the change of legal ownership. In May 1972, quotations were received for new type plates bearing the title 'London Country Bus Services' but this was not considered justifiable expenditure given the Country machines would all be gone within 2 years.

The rapid shedding of Country Gibsons led to a build up at Effra Road at this time and, for this reason, the overwhelming majority of surviving Gibsons that escaped decimalisation are to Country specification. London Country was requested to remove them but with no further use for the machines, it was agreed instead that they be sold to London Transport in 1975 for cannibalisation.

Above: In many respects this photograph symbolises why conductors lasted so much longer in London than anywhere else. Passengers appreciated tendering their fare to a human being and not a machine, while the short nature of most journeys meant that the faster loading times of crew operated routes gave them a distinct advantage in retaining passenger numbers and gathering revenue.
© TfL from the London Transport Museum collection

Right: Another factor in the existence of large numbers of conductors and their Gibsons well into the 1970s (and beyond) was the unreliability of new bus designs intended for one person operation. Obsolete vehicles like the RT type, shown here in Croydon in 1975, would not finally disappear until 1979. A change of policy in favour of crew operation in central London the following decade ensured the surviving Routemaster buses similarly had long service lives.

Ensuring everything was ready on 'D Day' was a logistical headache but of the minimum of 8200 Central Area Gibsons needed on the first day of decimal operation, an impressive 7522 were in place ready to be used fully decimalised (i.e. with a decimal fare strip and type wheel). The remainder had the dual fare strip fitted making them at least temporarily useable. All of these, as well as the spares and maintenance float, 9036 machines in all, had been fully decimalised by the end of March 1971.

There was no doubt that a substantial number of surplus Gibsons held in stock allowed much of the conversion work to take place well in advance. This, and the dedication of the staff involved, meant the change to decimal currency went extremely smoothly, so much so that D. Jones,

attending the Ticket Machine Works (Buses) meeting on the 23rd February 1971, representing M.J. McCoy, the Chief Operating Manager (Buses), was minuted as saying that he wanted placed on record his appreciation of the effort made by the Ticket Machine Works staff. Only 7 garages had to make do with dual fare strip machines on the due date which Mr Jones considered "most satisfactory". [6]

The Alpha Gibson
As the 1970s progressed, Britain entered the 'Winter of Discontent' and an ensuing financial crisis with high inflation caused prices to rise steeply. Inevitably this impacted on public transport fares. The Gibson's Achilles heel, the relative inflexibility in the face of changes in the fare scale, was starting

VALUE	ALPHA CODE	26 E	20 K
5 A	33 F	35 L	
8 B	36 G	28 M	
13 C	1 H	40 N	
21 D	10 J	45 P	

404/246   JUN 78

FARE PAID	CLASS	STAGE BOARDED
F	C/M	8 0

LONDON
TRANSPORT
38059

THIS TICKET IS AVAILABLE
FROM STAGE Nº INDICATED
ABOVE AND MUST BE SHOWN
ON DEMAND

ROUTE	TICKET Nº
316	3 9 9 7

NOT TRANSFERABLE

A P N M L K J H G F E D C B

to give cause for concern. After the fares increase of July 1977, the scale had only 2 points that corresponded to the 1971 Gibson decimal fare scale that remained in use. The other values required 'combination' tickets to 'build up' the necessary fare by the issue of 2, or in some cases, even 3 tickets. The high level of combination tickets required was impacting adversely on platform staff who found the extra work tiring and time consuming. Trade union pressure was mounting to modify the machines and stocks of ticket rolls were becoming depleted by the waste of paper by all the double issues. Normally a stock of 18 weeks' supply of rolls was kept in hand but, in spite of increased production, this had dropped to an all-time low of 11 weeks in December 1978.

A revised decimal range of 4p, 5p, 6p, 7p, 8p, 9p, 10p, 11p, 12p, 13p, 14p, 15p, 20p and 30p was proposed as the universal standard although an alternative plan was put forward to revisit the use of 'letter' or 'alpha' values, not used since the demise of the codes used to designate Early Morning Single issues. To accommodate fare revisions, the only alteration to the machine needed would be attachment of a new sticker externally informing the conductor what the corresponding cash equivalent was against each code.

Resistance to a coded fare system principally came again from the Traffic Audit Office worried that it presented opportunities for fraud, given the information printed on the ticket did not directly tell passengers what fare they had paid. The passengers themselves might be tempted to override too for the same reason. London Transport's Chief Public Relations Officer was not satisfied that sufficient prominence was being given to publicising the coded system when it was learnt information to passengers about the money equivalent of the new alpha codes was to be confined to the on board fare table only. The logical place to have this was on the back of the ticket but Effra Road lacked the means to produce printed rolls. The Chief Public Relations Officer's concerns were shared with the Chief Business Planning Officer, Ian Phillips; "permanent notices in the buses – perhaps at the expense of other material – is the price we should be prepared to pay for the advantages we gain from the change". Evidently there had been some concern over lost revenue from advertising space inside buses being given over to permanent notices on fare codes. [7]

There was the question too of the cost of converting the 6,700 Gibson machines still in use which was estimated at £30,000 and prohibitively expensive

Currency inflation throughout the 1970s meant regular fare increases and to cope, the alpha coding system was introduced in 1978, remaining in place until the end of Gibson operation. Changes in fares would henceforth only involve applying a different sticker to the top of the machine and altering publicity within the bus informing users what the new codes meant. Illustrated (top) are the first Alpha Gibson fare scale and sticker of June 1978, an Alpha fare strip (middle) and a ticket from Alpha machine no 38059 representing one of the highest so numbered due to the fitting of a new print plate to replace the worn-out original.

unless this could be seen as a 'once and for all' solution. With Union pressure mounting to do something about the double issues and with no feasible alternative in sight, the alpha coded system was reluctantly accepted, not only for the Gibson machine but also for the the 5230 'numeric' Almex E machines in use too, mostly on one-person buses.

The scale selected used capital letters A-H, J to N and P. The letters 'I' and 'O' were omitted to prevent confusion with numerals. Converting the decimal numeric Gibsons would take place at Effra Road at the rate of 200 a week but Almex E machines were given priority in the conversion programme as the impact of double-issue tickets was considered more onerous for driver-conductors.

The first garages to receive their Alpha Gibsons, on Sunday 13th August 1978, were Hackney and Wood Green and the last, Clapton and Upton Park, so converted on 26th August 1979. Work then turned to converting the maintenance float with all work completed by December 1979 – overall a total of 5920 machines were affected, less than anticipated due to continuing withdrawals.

The stickers applied to the machines were colour coded to make it evident the correct fare scale was being referred to by conductors. The June 1978 sticker was green and covered fares in a range between 5p and 45p with the higher values being reserved for fares on services extending beyond the GLC boundary. A further fare revision took place in 1979 when the sticker colour adopted was yellow and a maximum fare of 50p was adopted for code 'P'.

Most surviving Gibson machines today are of the alpha variety and outnumber surviving numeric decimalised machines at a ratio of about 7 to 1. To have escaped conversion to the alpha code indicates withdrawal from service prior to August 1979 and subsequent long term storage, typically as a source of spare parts.

The withdrawal programme

London Transport's Bus Reshaping Plan (BRP) of 1966 set out a very different blueprint for the future of the Capital's surface transport network to that of the 1940's, when the Gibson was designed, an era of mostly rear entrance double deck vehicles with fare collection by a roving conductor. The future envisaged a changed structure of routes based on major traffic objectives like railway stations and a much simpler fare scale, in some cases no scale at all with all passengers paying the same 'flat fare'. Significantly it envisaged the use of different types of vehicles with fewer seats and more floor space, capable of accommodating standing loads at peak times.

The BRP didn't initially propose widespread introduction of one person operation for inner London, which at that time was still not legally permissible for double deck vehicles using both decks. Moreover it was still seen as problematic in the Central Area, due to the short nature of passenger journeys (80% were two miles or less) and high levels of passenger traffic at peak periods, meaning congestion and unacceptably long journey times. But so too it was seen increasingly as the way forward in the face of a steady decline in passenger numbers due to car ownership, rising costs and staff shortages. Changes to the law in 1968 permitted one person operation of double deck buses to their full extent, but it was to high-capacity single deck buses that London Transport initially looked and a fare collection system that leant heavily in favour of 'self service' machines and turnstiles known as 'Automatic Fare Collection' (AFC). The influx of these buses, and development of the 'Londoner' or DMS class double deck equivalent from the late 1960s onwards, was intended to replace the ageing fleet of RT class buses and with them their conductors.

This steady decline in the number of crew-operated duties inevitably impacted the number of Gibson machines required for service. As early as 1959, it had been possible to supplant the TIM12s by Gibsons newly rendered surplus by a reduction in bus service frequencies. References then start to appear in the records of 'Authority to Withdraw Redundant Assets' (AWRA) authorisations, interestingly in the early period often in response to enquiries from abroad. One such example was the 100 Gibsons sold to Melbourne in 1959 at book price of £28 each which were needed to supplement a fleet of machines purchased new from TEL.

Allocation records have survived tracking this decline in Gibson numbers: in May 1969, 11,112 machines (including 1454 kept as spares) were required for service, falling to 8722 (including 1154 spare) in July 1971 and 6037 (including 924 spare) in March 1975. The last few Country Area machines were withdrawn in mid-1974 and, for some time, the practice continued of returning redundant Country machines to Effra Road which had built up a sizeable stockpile, 1200 machines in all. With their eventual sale to LT, most were broken up for spare parts although a very small number were allegedly prepared for road use by refitting route print wheels; the only clue to them being former Country Area machines would have been the 'route' reference ground off the type plate.

The use of Gibsons on scheduled bus services in central London didn't finally end until Saturday 21st August 1993 when routes 7 and 23 from Westbourne Park garage finally lost their allocation. The very last issue was apparently at the hand of Conductor Sharon Wieland on a route 7 journey using machine no 36694. The changeover was well documented by the media and featured on Carlton TV's 'London Tonight' programme, local radio and The Guardian newspaper. By that stage the Gibson machine was considered anachronistic; increasingly difficult to maintain and unsuited to computerised accounting methods. But a remarkable achievement none the less; an unprecedented 40 years of unbroken service since the first production machines appeared at Isleworth.

The Gibson in retrospect

Did the Gibson machine fulfil its design brief? The answer to that question was the subject of a report to the Executive Board in April 1957 when the mechanisation programme was virtually complete. The report concluded that introducing Gibson machines had:

a) Reduced the incidence of uncollected fares, especially at the minimum fare level where typically passengers rode only one or two stops;

b) In respect of higher fare values, passengers are served sooner after boarding so obtain a ticket for the full length of the journey rather than just the remaining section once the conductor can reach them;

c) The conductor has more time to supervise passengers and therefore discourage overriding;

d) Less need to collect fares as passengers alight therefore reducing the temptation for fraud.

In December 1979, only 4872 Gibson machines were needed for service (including 742 held as spare) and it seemed inevitable the end would soon come. But a change of policy away from wholesale one person operation and 'AFC' in central London, and a recognition that crew operation had a future, brought about a reprieve. While numbers continued to slowly decline throughout the 1980s, it is remarkable that any Gibson machines at all were required for service at the dawn of the 1990s.

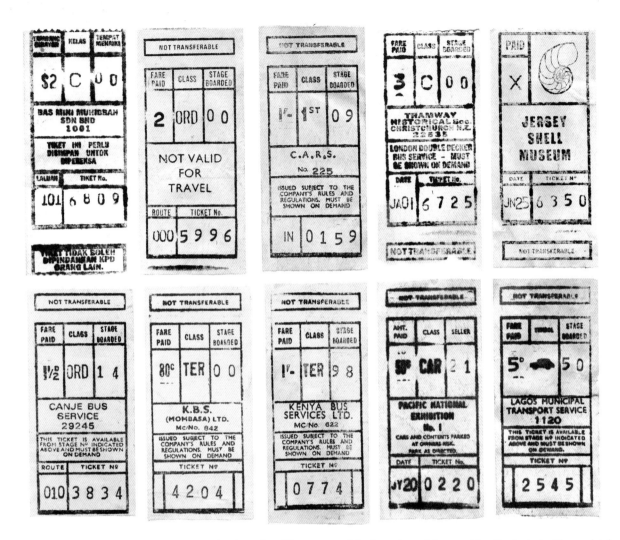

Opposite page: London Transport began disposals of surplus Gibsons surprisingly early and the machine illustrated with unmistakeable London heritage spent more years in service in Nyasaland (now Malawi) than in the Capital. The homemade fare selector knob replaced the ebonite original which was prone to damage by knocks. An advertising slogan incorporated in the print plate—in this case for Coca-Cola—was a novel feature not adopted in London. The 'super-short' style of print plate was a logical development in an effort to keep paper consumption to a bare minimum in markets where obtaining supplies of ticket rolls might be difficult.

Above: The tickets above illustrate the diversity of Gibson disposals, mostly bus operators in what was still at the time Britain's colonies. Unfortunately, little is known of the operators that used them. The machine from Lagos is interesting, having a wide fare print wheel fitted that showed a symbol alongside the fare value to assist recognition. Other users included the Pacific National Exhibition in Vancouver, the shell museum in Jersey and the Tramway Historical Society of Christchurch, New Zealand. The latter machine accompanied RT 3132 which journeyed to New Zealand in conjunction with participation of the England team at the 1974 Commonwealth Games and stayed.

These assertions were substantiated by a survey entitled 'Uncollected Fares and Excess Riding (Road Services)' undertaken in 1956 that found uncollected fares on routes using Gibson machines was 20% lower than on routes still using bell punches. The ability of conductors to have both hands free meant both speed and a greater margin of safety in a moving vehicle although, interestingly, no study seems to have been commissioned examining accidents both amongst staff and passengers and whether or not Gibson introduction had helped here too. Certainly there was anecdotal evidence to suggest conductors with Gibsons spent more time on the platform, thus enabling them to better supervise passengers boarding and alighting from the bus and, with it, the potential to reduce accidents.

Principal drawbacks when compared to the punch system were that passengers were less aware of the face value of their ticket, as issues from a machine lacked the distinctive colour coding of pre-printed tickets that immediately

Above left: The manufacturer's tag from an early Gibson when TEL was under the wing of the Rothschild empire and manufacture based at Tring.

Middle: After the sale of TEL to TIM Ltd in 1956, production moved to Cirencester and later machines and spare parts carried this simpler style of label. By this time, interest in the machine was waning and it was not even thought significant for the tag to carry patent information.

identified the fare they represented. And of course the problem of the lack of adaptability to fare increases, or more properly 'fare revisions' as they were euphemistically referred to, featured large in the report.

The 1957 report gives us a detailed insight into fare collection in the Capital at the peak of Gibson usage as shown in Tables 1 and 2 (below). These allow some tentative calculations based on the number of tickets issued throughout the lifetime of a machine. Making the assumption that a machine had a full service life beginning in 1954 and not leaving service until 1992, this equates to a staggering 7.3 million issues. And this does not make allowance for combination issues, so another 10–20% could realistically be added to this figure.

Since no report to the Executive would be complete without a financial appraisal, the total outlay to purchase the 17,000 Gibson machines was £608,600 (over £16 million in today's terms). Table 3 (below) sets out the estimated annual running costs:

The staff establishment at the time these figures were produced was 196 Output Assistants. This compared favourably to the far larger numbers of people preparing, processing and distributing punch ticket boxes. The Output Assistants were expected to process 95 machines per day, which involved preparing them for service (ensuring the route and where appropriate date was set, entering the opening readings on the waybill and ensuring a pack of emergency tickets was provided) and then checking them back in at the end of the duty. Production costs for ticket rolls, which were largely manufactured in-house, were also considerably cheaper than for punch tickets. The 1957 report concluded "the mechanisation of the ticket service has undoubtedly improved the efficiency of fare collection....the Gibson machine has shown itself to be eminently suitable for the conditions on the Executive's bus services but is at some disadvantage in dealing with frequently changing fare values". [8]

Table 1 – Gibson Machine requirements (assuming 'TIM12's are replaced) as at April 1957 (1 per duty for Central Area)

	Central Bus	Trolleybus	Country Bus	Total
No. of duties (Mon-Fri)	11,172	2,705	1,613	15,490
2½% duty spares	280	68	40	388
3% defective spares	335	81	49	465
Green Line coach duplicates	-	-	241	241
Maintenance float	295	72	80	447
			TOTAL	17,031

Table 2 – Estimated paper consumption per year based on 1957 (1000s)

	Central Bus	Trolleybus	Country Bus	Total
Estimated no. of tickets issued	2,307,000	656,000	281,000	3,244,000
Ticket rolls consumed	6,706	1,907	817	9,430

Table 3 – Estimated annual cost of operating Gibson machines to April 1957

	Central Bus	Trolleybus	Country Bus	Total
Interest and depreciation	£51,000	£12,400	£8,500	£71,900
Maintenance costs (repairs, servicing, inking etc.)	£80,300	£19,400	£9,300	£109,000
Ticket rolls	£51,300	£14,600	£6,250	£72,150
Waybill printing costs	£2,300	£500	£300	£3,100
Garage and depot based office staff	£96,000	£24,500	£17,700	£138,200
Traffic audit staff	£3,700	£1,300	-	£5,000
Transport	£5,000	£1,300	£1,700	£8,000
TOTAL	£289,600	£74,000	£43,750	£407,350

Afterlife

As was the case with London buses, many of the withdrawn Gibson machines in the early days, still with plenty of service life left in them, readily found homes with other operators. Mention has been made of the machines that went to Australia. In April 1959 due to "a favourable opportunity for their sale" 84 redundant Gibsons (with a book value of £2289) were sold to an unknown buyer, possibly the Nyasaland Transport Company which maintained links with London Transport.[9] Another 80 went to the Lagos Transport Company in October that year, no doubt others were to follow as Lagos was a large Gibson user and the London Transport Staff Magazine of December 1959 refers to Senior Instructor Frederick Williams of Chiswick Training School spending 3 months in Lagos instructing staff of the Lagos Municipal Transport in the use of Gibsons. Prior to this no form of ticketing was in use. Machines were still being shipped there as late as 1991.

TEL themselves approached London Transport in 1959 to see if they would sell them back 100 machines, presumably in response to another overseas enquiry. In October 1966, the Ceylon Transport Board wanted to buy surplus machines and in 1967 the unusual use of surplus London Gibsons was being explored by Corona Soft Drinks Ltd, for some unidentified purpose.

The Seaton & District Electric Tramway enquired about using 15 modified Gibsons for tramway use in February 1973 but there is no record whether or not any were supplied. No significant number of surplus London Gibson machines found further use with British bus operators. Those other UK operators that did use Gibsons bought them new from TEL.

Above: As thoughts turned to a replacement machine for the Gibson, this is what the future of ticketing in London might have looked like in 1957: the unique Pearson machine with punched paper audit roll and (left), a sample ticket. Only one was built, ostensibly for evaluation purposes, but the emergence of a more suitable alternative to punched paper to record statistical data, in the form of magnetic tape, brought about the project's abrupt demise.

The Search for a Replacement

The Gibson A14 was by all expectations an outstanding success. Getting it into production had taken far longer than anticipated, but the machine proved reliable in service and came to be much loved by staff who liked, amongst other qualities, the ability to issue tickets from either end of the machine by using the handle or spinning the fare knob (though this practice was officially frowned upon as it was thought to cause excessive wear to the machine's bearings) with obvious appeal to left handed users. Changing ticket rolls was simple and while the process of cashing in at duty end by adding the totals of 14 individual fare counters was laborious, there was certainty and immediacy in the results.

But the machine's weaknesses were apparent too, not just the thorny problem over fare changes but also the limited fare range. A report to the Executive in 1959 stated the Gibson is "not entirely satisfactory and involves a great deal of clerical work by garage staff in preparing the machines and cash total sheets and by the conductors in the preparation of cash total sheets, which in turn have to be checked in detail". What was wanted was "a completely new system in which the issuing machine used by the conductor and the subsequent office routines shall all form an integrated whole"[1]

This vision for the future was made possible by technological advances, not just in the sophistication of the machines themselves but through the growing use of electronics and early computer technology to revolutionise back office processes and in particular the gathering and analysis of traffic data. The 1959 report set out the design features of the likely Gibson replacement machine:

a) Retain the existing speed of issue and be at least as lightweight;

b) Sufficiently wide coverage of the range of fare values for the foreseeable future and the ability to issue tickets at any half fare value;

c) Provide a 'tally roll' from which statistical analysis is possible by fare value and the number of tickets issued from any given fare stage;

d) A total tickets issued counter which will print on suitable documents such as a waybill.

Only one machine on the market at the time met all but the last of these requirements; the Almex Model A which had been developed in Sweden in the late 1940s and introduced into Britain in partnership with neighbouring Maidstone & District Motor Services which had been successfully using them since 1957 on one person buses. A machine was duly loaned and examined by E.C. Ottaway, the Chief Supplies & Services Officer in April 1959. He dismissed it though as unsuitable for London use because of the rather involved process in changing ticket rolls, the lack of duplicate cumulative cash counters and the fact it weighed more than a Gibson machine. He baulked too on grounds of cost which was in the region of £100 apiece, three times the cost of a Gibson. The need for a second set of cash counters was seen as important to validate the machine was functioning correctly in the inevitable event of disputes over conductors paying in 'unders'. [2]

The Pearson patents
It is clear work on a possible Gibson replacement at the Ticket Machine Works at Effra Road was progressing even as the last Gibsons were being received from the TEL factory at Cirencester (TEL had become part of TIM Ltd shortly before). The main player here was a member of staff at Effra Road, Alfred Pearson, who, in much the same way George Gibson had done before him, patented his innovative designs jointly with his employer for what was hoped to be the next generation of ticket equipment. The idea was to produce a design combining the portability and ease of use of the Gibson with the capability of a wide range of fare values.

Key was the ability of the machine to produce an audit tally so a wide range of data from ticket sales could be captured for later analysis. This meant cash counters only need record the total value of all ticket sales so that the necessary reconciliation against what the conductor had paid in could be done. The audit tally would allow back up in case of disputes and also statistical analysis.

and another, (714161 - 8473/51) filed by Licenta Patent-Verwaltungs (LPW) G.m.b.H. of Hamburg. Both covered similar ground in that they were for machines able to issue tickets or vouchers with an audit tally, but otherwise were not sufficiently similar. The Siemens invention relied on an audit tally in the form of a serrated paper roll but the patent itself had been allowed to lapse. The LPW produced printed characters on the tally roll but with the novel feature that this was contained in a readily removable box. This allowed data from separate duties to be readily collected, with the additional advantage that it allowed the machine to remain in use while the earlier record was being analysed.

Initially it was thought punched paper technology could provide the answer to a portable ticket machine incorporating an audit tally roll. Technology was now sufficiently advanced that perforated paper was readily readable by a suitable device linked to a

This idea of incorporating a tally roll in a machine for London use was not new. In June 1938 a design by a Major AP Hodges came to the Board's attention for a "portable conductor's ticket machine issuing pre-printed tickets and to record automatically the ticket issue on a duplicated record strip". It showed sufficient promise for authority to be given for a budget of £250 to be set aside for the manufacture of a prototype and the Board's Solicitor (General) asked to draw up a suitable agreement on similar lines to the later one with George Gibson. Nothing further appears to have been done and within a year Britain was at war, so the project was quietly shelved.[3]

Before significant development work could proceed, as before with the Gibson, existing patents had to be checked to make sure there were no infringements of already patented inventions. This uncovered an old 1930s Siemens patent (442314 - 32497/34)

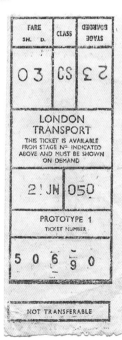

computer. Using this approach, patent 843029 - 38225/57 was duly applied for jointly by the BTC on behalf of the Executive and Pearson in 1957, and approved by the Patent Office in March 1959. With an unmistakeable Gibson heritage, a solitary prototype machine was built and numbered 15000, the type plate clearly adapted from the one originally intended for the first standard machine short plate conversion. Fare range was from ½d to 6/11½d and, in accordance with the 1959 specification, incorporated the innovative feature of being able to print the total cash counter readings on a suitably inserted card or waybill. In spite of these advanced features, it proved far too heavy for anything other than bulkhead mounting in a one person bus. The operation of the paper punching device too would have proved problematic in service, quickly clogging up with paper debris.

In the event punch tape technology for a portable ticket machine proved a dead end, but in the form of a subsequent patent (880933 – 1929/59 also jointly between BTC and Pearson), a more promising design emerged using printed characters on the tally roll. Two experimental machines were produced, built entirely by hand at the Effra Road works in the 1959-1961 period at an estimated cost of £5000 (£110,000 in today's terms), utilising much of the spare parts bin from the Gibson machine. Indeed in overall appearance, the machines produced looked very much like a Gibson, but a bank of fare selectors allowed tickets to be produced in a range from 1d to 3/11d in 1d steps. Two sets of cash counters recorded pence and shillings values and, despite the inclusion of these features, the machine was creditably light.

In response to the Board's ticket machine requirements (London Transport Executive had been replaced by the London Transport Board in 1962), two external manufacturers submitted designs too using a printed internal audit roll in keeping with Pearson's ideas. One was Bell Punch Ltd, which built two machines with the designation P51, one with a tally roll consisting of a pattern of dots, the other with conventional printed characters. The other firm responding was the manufacturer of the Gibson, TEL Ltd, now fully absorbed by TIM Ltd, which submitted one machine that produced a single line of printed characters on the audit tally much in the way the Almex A machine did. The P51 proved far too heavy and bulky to be carried and proved unreliable on test. The rejection of these machines caused Bell Punch to abandon the project and, intriguingly, this appears to be the company's only foray into producing a roll ticket machine other than the Ultimate.

The TEL prototype showed greater potential but as optical character reading equipment in the early 1960s was still relatively primitive, variations in the density of the print impression on the audit tally roll meant the data couldn't be reliably extracted for processing by a computer.

Pearson's third invention was jointly developed in association with EMI Electronics Ltd of Hayes, Middlesex, using magnetic tape technology in lieu of a paper roll for the audit tally. EMI made two patent applications (37778/60 and 3357/61) for a small and compact EMF generator using a bank of permanent magnets to produce a signature on the tape surface as it was passed over them. Cams engaging these magnets allowed them to either touch the tape surface or retract from it, depending on the variables for the ticket selected; fare, stage, class etc.

The 'Magnetic Tally Generator', or MTG as it came to be known, used removable compact tape cassettes specially developed for data capture purposes in conjunction with a designated reader linked to a computer. The MTG unit and cassettes were cheap to produce and worked reliably as no electronic circuitry or power source was required.

The story of the subsequent extensive field trials with a range of ticket machines using magnetic tape technology is fascinating in its own right but, except in passing, is beyond the scope of this book. It did look though, as the 1960s progressed, that magnetic tape designs produced by TEL, and later Setright (as its SM.D model machine) and Almex with an offshoot of the Model A known as the A.763, might provide the answer to London's future bus ticketing needs. Extensive service trials took place from 1967 onwards but unfortunately, for a variety of reasons, none of them proved satisfactory as a Gibson replacement.

Left page: The Gibson prototype machine built at Effra Road and subsequently adapted to incorporate the MTG unit developed in conjunction with EMI. A stepped fare range was provided covering every value from 1d to 3/11d. Illustrated are tickets from this machine (left), another Gibson prototype machine, for which no written records exist (centre) and the production MTG TEL machine (right).

Repeated problems were encountered with the zeroing cumulative cash counter specified by London Transport and manufactured by English Numbering Machines. This gave rise to a growing incidence of staff disputes over takings. This and quality control issues generally, made worse by the use of nylon of the incorrect specification for gears, meant a high proportion of machines received from the factory failed their pre-service checks and had to be returned. Despite much hard work on both sides to address the problems, the Setright company asked to be relieved of its contractual obligations in September 1969 when only 120 of the order for 200 SM.Ds had been delivered. These were all returned to Setright minus their MTG units when their replacements, 200 standard SM.B Mk II machines, were received in late 1969.

The dalliance with magnetic tape technology for its ticket machines had cost London Transport dearly, something in the region of £195,000 (£3.5 million today) by July 1968.[4] At that point the need was recognised to hit the pause button on developing bespoke solutions to the Board's ticketing

By 1971 the trial had ended, with the only concrete conclusion that a clear winner had emerged in the form of the Almex machine in terms of performance and reliability, but it proved too heavy to be carried by a conductor. Ideally suited for static mounting, they found a useful niche equipping pay as you enter Green Line coaches. Indeed, in addition to the 200 trial machines, a further batch of 120 A.763s was received in 1969 and subsequently another 250 to decimal currency specification in 1971, all for use in the Country Area. Subsequent orders were for the standard Almex Model A machine, without the MTG unit, and large numbers were taken to introduce 'single manning' throughout the green bus network.

The 50 offerings from TEL received from October 1967 initially had mixed fortunes and began life at Harlow before settling at Godstone garage where they remained. Conductors on route 410 would have encountered Central Area colleagues using the Almex A.763 machines in crew mode on route 227 at Bromley until weight issues prevented their further use in that capacity. In spite of a poor record for reliability, the TELs soldiered on until the advent of decimal currency when they were withdrawn by London Country and offered back to London Transport, which had no further use for them.

The Setright 'SM.D' proved the most problematic; delivery was over 12 months late as the factory evidently struggled with adapting the design to the London specification.

Above: Tickets from the Almex A.763 (left) and (right), from the numeric version of the Almex E. Like its Gibson counterpart, rapid increases in fares meant the need for the Almex E to later adopt an alpha fare coded system similarly involving the need for internal modifications to the machine.

Left: The production TEL machine was nicknamed 'the plastic Gibson' due to the extensive use of moulded parts.

Opposite page: The eventual winner of the 1968 trial was the Almex A.763 and cemented a successful future partnership with the Swedish manufacturer. A change machine is also seen in use on this RF class vehicle, recently upgraded for continued use on Green Line routes.

needs given large scale change was being proposed, namely wider use in London of one person operation and the growing momentum in favour of Automatic Fare Collection (AFC). This was in part a response to London Transport's own 'Bus Reshaping Plan' but also a realisation that the newly introduced Bus Grant to speed up one person operation on grounds of efficiency also extended to some AFC equipment where it was a permanent installation feature. These changes happened relatively quickly and it meant fewer conductors would be needed and an ever larger pool of surplus Gibson machines could be made available. Through a process of cannibalisation, these could yield spare parts very cost-effectively to keep the remainder going. Indeed a memorandum of 1973 on the subject of how long Gibson machines could be kept operational concluded that the 5500 machines needed that

year could be maintained until at least 1977 from the spare parts stock. The only spares in urgent need of replenishment were type plates which for all 5500 machines would cost in the region of £11,000 but was never acted upon at that level. While undoubtedly some Gibsons did receive new type plates quite late in the day, the majority had to make do as evident by the deteriorating legibility of printed tickets as the years passed.

Before leaving the subject of the trial machines, mention should be made of the fate of the two experimental Gibson machines built at Effra Road which aptly were christened 'Prototype 1' and 'Prototype 2'. Initially, one machine retained the paper audit tally and the other was rebuilt to incorporate the new MTG unit. In these respective formats

they were put to work in field trials during April 1962 from Brixton garage alongside two experimental TEL machines, 00001 (MTG) and 00002 (with a paper roll audit facility). In June 1962 they were joined by an adapted Almex Model A machine capable of recording data on magnetic tape by which time both the Gibson machines had the MTG unit. The trial ended in October 1962 and resumed with modified TEL and Almex machines the following year on route 50 from Streatham garage, but by this stage the Gibson experiment had concluded. Newer and better designs had presented themselves and developing the Gibson platform further to incorporate the additional requirement for a cumulative and zeroing cash counter was not considered economically justified.

MODEL E

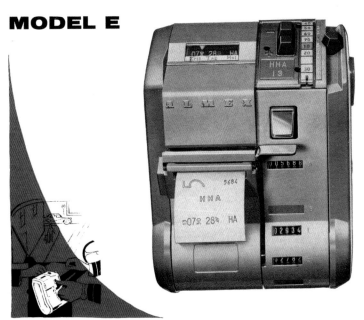

ALMEX

FOR TOWN TRAFFIC

ALMEX new ticket machine for town traffic — model E — is extremely fast in operation, provides an efficient control and clear statistical information. The machine prints the Company's name, fare, serial number, time, stage, line etc. on blanks or part printed rolls. It can be fitted with counters for up to 9 different fare values and if required can also cancel return and weekly tickets. There are 2 total counters for number of passengers and for tickets issued. The machine is operated simply and quickly with one hand only. The machine is equally suitable for portable or stationary use.

The Almex Model E

While the love affair between London Country and the Almex Model A was only just beginning, London Transport was still no further forward in identifying a replacement for its aging Gibson machines. Likewise it still lacked a suitable candidate to equip its new fleet of one person operated high capacity single deck buses and the intended replacement to the Routemaster, the Daimler Fleetline DMS class. Hitherto, routes converted to one-person operation had relatively simple fare scales reflecting the limitations of the Ultimate machine. London Transport had amassed 781 of these by May 1973, some of them migrants from London Country. Bolstered by the success of the Almex machine in the various trials of the 1960s, but unconvinced the Model A or its derivative was the right machine for the job, the focus of attention turned to a new machine from Almex, the Model E. Developed in the 1960s specifically for urban transportation systems, it had the hitherto elusive distinction of being equally at home on pay as you enter buses as well as gracing the shoulders of a conductor.

Rather unusually, the Board didn't commission the type of comparative field trials that had characterised the introduction of new types of machines in the previous decades. Instead, it opted for a trial batch of 18 Model E machines which were deployed at Hounslow in 1969. Others followed, swelling the total to 110 by July 1970. Hard on the heels of this was a bulk order of 758 machines intended for one person operation in conjunction with the 1970 vehicle purchase programme. This consisted of 300 single deck and 100 double deck buses, all but 42 being to a 'split entrance' layout to enable passengers to be streamed towards use of AFC equipment or to pay their fare conventionally to the driver, who would be equipped with an

Above: The Almex E first appeared in the 1960s to meet the need of urban transport systems where rapidity of operation was more a priority than the fare range, limited as it was to only 9 values. Over 6500 were purchased by London Transport over a 10 year period. The model above, with central operating lever, was suitable for carriage by a conductor, while the example opposite is shown on its motorised base for bulkhead mounting and use by the driver on one person operated vehicles.

Almex E machine. The Bus Reshaping Plan, which was driving these developments, meant that never before had vehicle and ticketing requirements been so closely allied but the sense of urgency would spell problems ahead.

The lack of thorough testing caused a wobble in August 1970 when a growing number of defects brought London Transport to the point of seriously considering abandoning the Almex E altogether in favour of Ultimate machines for its 1970/71 intake of 1125 units. This would very much have been a backward step and in the event, the Almex company proved attentive to correcting the faults and modifications were made to improve reliability. The order duly fell on Almex and the Model E, all intended for pay as you enter use by mounting on a purpose designed motorised base unit also marketed by Almex. [5]

The machine was supplied by Almex in one of two different formats; the first purely as a manually operated machine with the lever responsible for ticket issue amidships and in direct alignment with the release button. In this guise though it couldn't be married to the motorised base unit for powered ticket issue most suited for one person operation. The second variant, and the one London Transport mostly opted for, was designed for use on this base unit with drive take up on the side panel of the machine. It was, however, still possible to use the machine manually by attaching a screw on handle but it was a rather flimsy affair and only intended for emergency use in the event the base unit failed. The only way in which the two types of machines could be made interchangeable was by modification by the manufacturer or at the Ticket Machine Works.

The relevance of all this to the Gibson story is that, by default, the Almex E became the ticket machine of choice as it was adopted as the standard for one person operation, either in conjunction with 'AFC' or as a stand-alone application.

A drawing back from the wholesale adoption of one person operation caused by the adverse public response to boarding times prompted a rethink and a proposal was put forward in September 1973 to convert 500 of the 2780 Model E machines thus far delivered to manual configuration as Gibson replacements, at an estimated cost of £5,770. Having to reconfigure machines barely a couple of years old shows the state of flux in transport planning circles at the time.

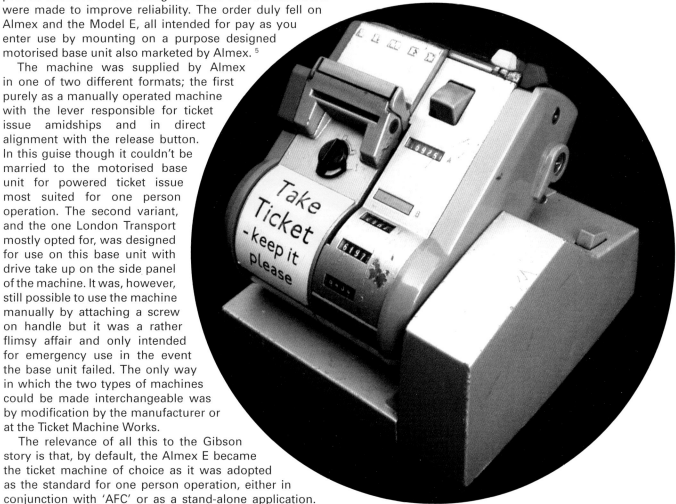

The first documented use of Almex E machines in conductor use was in 1974 when, as a pilot, 30 converted machines were supplied for route 261 at Palmers Green in preference to Gibsons. In April 1974, the trial moved to routes 298A and 29, the latter on Sundays only. In October 1974 it was the turn of Kingston for weekday use on route 71 and Sundays on route 65. Palmers Green was allowed to revert to Gibson operation.

It seemed by the close of 1974, the position of the 'manual' Almex E machine was assured as a Gibson replacement, to the extent that development work was begun with the Swedish company to develop a Data Capture Device. It seemed the ideas behind the earlier MTG trials had something of a rejuvenation by the development of a transistorised device to simplify data capture and transfer. In the event, London Transport did not invest further in the project, perhaps sensing the pace of technology was rapidly advancing in favour of integrated circuit electronics and the possibilities for transport applications these offered.

Any intended wholesale displacement of Gibson machines at this point seems to have drawn breath. It has to be said, in exchange for their trusted Gibson, an Almex E was not particularly welcomed by conductors, indeed their use at Palmers Green had resulted in a Union ultimatum to remove them as 50% of the staff there apparently thought them unreliable. It seems the change of use did bring into gaze a further round of technical problems with the Almex machine. While not insurmountable, it set a few heads scratching at Effra Road when it was thought most of the earlier Almex gremlins had been exorcised. [6]

Deliveries of Almex E machines intended for one person operation continued unabated meanwhile, supplanting the last Ultimates in February 1978, and the 1977/78 intake of 800 Model Es included 200 manual machines. This had more to do with the intended new Universal Bus Ticketing experiment centred on Havering than a network-wide move to replace Gibsons. It was hoped the experiment then underway at Havering would see a move away from fares payment for single journeys to pre-purchase of multi-ride travel at a discount.

By September 1978, manual Almex E machines could be found in use for crew operated Havering scheme routes emanating from Barking, Romford (North Street), Seven Kings and Upton Park garages which were now all-Almex. [7] Allocation records for October 1979 show manual Model E machines also in use at Plumstead, Hanwell, Kingston, Norbiton and Uxbridge garages, a total of 492 in all, both purchased new as manual machines and conversions.

This represents the high water mark of the Almex E as a Gibson replacement though: the same number are recorded in April 1981 but this had fallen back to just 296 two years later. What had caused this rethink in replacing the increasingly out-dated Gibson with a modern alternative? The problem was not Trade Union opposition: indeed after that initial reluctance at Palmers Green, the Model E became accepted as the inevitable Gibson successor. A second phase of Gibson to Almex conversions was proposed in September 1978 with an 'open ended' order for 900 machines at a total cost of £286,000 (£1.7 million today) but tellingly, in spite of the financial incentives to do so, the Board was not prepared to commit to replacing all 7000 Gibson machines in use at the time with a long term contract with Almex. This order was subsequently scaled back to just 300 items. The reason for this was that even in the late 'seventies it was known that a new generation of electronic machines was in development that might question the wisdom of so far-sighted a commitment. It seemed too Gibsons could be kept serviceable long enough to see London Transport through the twilight years of crew operation, by which time even modern mechanical ticket machines, like the Almex, might themselves be considered obsolete. [8]

The final chapter of the Gibson to Almex conversion programme was one of reversal: in many cases, manual Model E machines for crew operation were withdrawn in favour of Gibsons which were in plentiful supply. This was a strange turn of events and reflected a trend that would gather momentum by repurposing old and trusted designs like the Routemaster and the Gibson in favour of wholesale replacement. So much so in fact that by October 1983 all the manual Model Es had gone, having been converted for use on driver only routes other than a handful used on a stand for one person operated Airbus services from Central London to Heathrow Airport.

Into the 1990s

Therefore there seemed little point as the 1980s progressed looking for a Gibson replacement machine which need last no longer than London Transport would retain crew operation, surely no more than a few years at the most. This turned out to be rather more protracted than originally thought. The turmoil caused by privatisation of bus routes in London and growing public attachment to rear platform buses in the Capital would see a reprieve for the Routemaster in the new decade. This was made possible by the vehicle's rugged construction meaning modern engineering components could be grafted to the composite body structure, substantially extending life expectancy.

A rethink too was needed on the life expectancy of the remaining Gibsons in service, as crew worked buses seemed to be here to stay. Theoretically the remaining Gibsons could be kept going virtually indefinitely: continued cannibalisation of surplus machines would yield most of the needed parts, leaving a relatively small number of newly sourced or remanufactured components needed to keep the fleet serviceable. But this didn't solve the lack of an interface with computerised revenue accounting and management systems which were increasingly becoming the norm. A partial solution was found by the inclusion of Gibson cash total sheets within the new computerised accounting system and by March 1988 all garages were using this in preference to the previous Bus Accounting & Revenue System (BARC). This allowed integration with the new generation of driver operated electronic ticket machines (ETMs) then entering service but Gibson data input was still largely a manual process.

The Portable Electronic Ticket Machine (PETM)

In May 1985, ETM trials began on one person operated routes at Loughton and Finchley garages and at Palmers Green from that November, using proprietary electronic products provided by three different companies. A fully operational trial followed in October 1986 at Plumstead using Wayfarer ETMs, the machine subsequently chosen for the main conversion programme of one person operated routes from late 1986 onwards at a rate of three garages per month, concluding in March 1988 when the last Almex machines were withdrawn.

A proven case had been made for the ETM to Almex changeover, but at that time "no manufacturer so far has indicated that an economic and practical replacement

portable electronic machine will be available".[9] This meant, in the absence of suitable electronic replacement for the Gibson, the remaining 4352 machines still in service in 1985 would have to soldier on a bit longer.

Above: The Gibson is no more when this view was taken in 1994. Pictured is Mrs Madge Chambers with her Wayfarer 'Clipper' PETM. Route 22 would retain its Routemasters until July 2005.
© TfL from the London Transport Museum collection

While the passing of the Gibson ticket machine was mourned in many circles, latterly it had proved expensive to maintain and 'making do' became the norm as evidenced by the number of surviving machines with parts such as handles that were crudely repaired rather than replaced.

After the compulsory tendering of engineering facilities, Gibson maintenance had been taken on by Bus Engineering Ltd (BEL) from 1988 and this one activity represented a significant chunk of their business. This arrangement left London Buses Ltd (the post deregulation successor organisation to public ownership of buses in London) vulnerable to having to rely on a single maintenance outlet to keep their Gibson machines going. That outlet could cease operations or substantially increase costs with impunity. There was very little other choice of maintenance facilities as manual ticket equipment, and the industry that supported it, was rapidly becoming a thing of the past. With very few moving parts, Clipper maintenance was based more on the replacement of faulty parts and circuit boards, not the laborious task of stripping the machine down, cleaning and checking each component and then rebuilding it: operations that had characterised Gibson maintenance.

Clippers had the advantage too of infinite flexibility in ticket configuration and pricing and the wealth of information on ticket sales could be freely transcribed using a computer interface to a level unimaginable 25 years before. The lack of this data by the continuing use of Gibson machines was identified as a factor in the late tendering of central London bus routes. To save weight, the memory module in the Clipper was integral and not readily removable; data download took place when the machine itself was docked to a suitable reader and charging point.

But in the hearts of the travelling public, the PETMs were not as fondly regarded and the staff too had occasion at times to bemoan the loss of their Gibson when the battery on their Clipper ran flat as they were inclined to do with heavy usage.

With the likelihood that crewed bus operations outside London would soon become extinct as the decade progressed, no manufacturer had thus far developed a suitable portable electronic ticket machine. As a result, a development contract was entered into with Wayfarer Transit Systems Ltd of Poole, Dorset (London Buses ETM supplier) to produce one. A live trial using 5 prototype portable ETMs (known as 'PETM's) took place on routes 11 and 19 from Victoria garage in February and March 1991. The proposed programme would see the first pilot garage conversion in December 1991. The main phase of introduction would be from April 1992 onwards, concluding, it was proposed, in January 1993, so replacing all 1900 Gibsons estimated as remaining in use at that date.[10]

The trial with the experimental PETMs certainly proved to be a success and the contract to replace the last Gibsons was awarded to Wayfarer in September 1991 to supply the machines, known now as the 'Clipper'. From November 1992 when Clippers first appeared at Tottenham garage for route 73, one by one all 16 garages still operating two person crewed routes lost their Gibson machines, concluding with Westbourne Park in August 1993. Details of the conversion programme are included in Appendix 6.

WAYFARER CLIPPER

WAYFARER ARE PROUD TO ANNOUNCE AN ADDITION TO THEIR ELECTRONIC TICKETING FAMILY.

A LIGHTWEIGHT PORTABLE ELECTRONIC TICKETING MACHINE.

In the traffic congested areas of our cities, even the shortest of stops can affect operating efficiency. If you are concerned about losing time, switch to the Wayfarer Clipper and reduce the waiting time on your routes. With the fastest ticket issuing machine in the west (or the east for that matter), Wayfarer offer you a step forward into tomorrow !

- A lightweight portable ticketing machine which is fast, accurate and reliable, using two high speed 9 needle print heads and proven ink bobbin printing.

- Simple to operate and maintain

- Robust and compact design, using state-of-the art technology.

- Up to 20 preset tickets and classes and 9,999 'open' settings.

- Built in magnetic card swipe reader and smart card option.

- Suitable for use on buses, trams, ferries, trains, underground and metro systems.

- Handles a variety of tickets - single issue, multi-journey, returns and passes.

- Simple paper loading.

- Extended battery life - 14 hours or 1000 tickets before recharge.

IF YOU'RE ISSUING TICKETS, IT MUST BE WAYFARER

070328   23 421 17:18 05JUN01 £1.00 Adult

London Buses Not transferable Retain ticket for inspection   London Buses Not transferable Retain ticket for inspection   London Buses Not transferable Retain ticket for inspection

4738   Valid to Liverpool St. Stn. (57)

Previous page top: A prototype, now in the Acton museum, of the PETM developed by Wayfarer as the machine to replace the final Gibsons in London service.

This page, below and left: The production machine, branded the 'Clipper' and publicity material issued by the manufacturer, Wayfarer Transit Systems Ltd of Poole, Dorset. The fare selector and manner in which ticket rolls were loaded was reminiscent of Gibson practice.

Bottom left: A sample ticket from a later machine. The alighting point to which the fare had been paid was a novel feature and helped deter overriding. (Photographs courtesy of Damon Cross)

Provincial Gibsons

Mention has been made of London Transport Gibson machines rendered surplus that found new homes with overseas operators. In addition, Crawley Ticket Machines, and later TEL, endeavoured to market the machine in their own right. Undoubtedly a better designed and executed product than the TIM, the short fare range meant it was entering a very crowded marketplace, one dominated by the industry giants Bell Punch Ltd with its Ultimate model and TIM Ltd, with an unassailable lead established from the 1930s onwards.

The biggest order for Gibson A14 machines outside London came from Melbourne in Australia, where the Melbourne & Metropolitan Tramways Board bought new long plate machines from TEL as well as, later, ex-London short plate variants—the last in 1965. A total fleet of 450 was built up over a number of years.

Gibsons were also supplied in long plate form (i.e. no later than 1956) to Douglas Corporation on the Isle of Man which took at least 60 machines and to Accrington Corporation who had a smaller number, perhaps no more than 20, as they were also TIM users. After the introduction

of the shorter type plate, West Bridgford Urban District Council purchased a small batch of machines, again in the region of 20, which were to an unusual dual fare layout. Fare values were prefixed with a 'W' for West Bridgford, 'C' for Nottingham Corporation and 'T' for through routes to enable takings to be apportioned appropriately between the two neighbouring municipal operators.

The West Bridgford machines were also unusual in that they featured a revised actuating method to enable the handle to be turned. The handle assembly had a skirted housing and the knob pushed downwards to release the catch rather than the more familiar catch arrangement on the top of the machine. This may have been to make the machine more acceptable to TIM users who were used to having the release catch in close proximity to the handle, a more logical arrangement. Perhaps too it was seen as a step towards use of the machine on a fixed base for one person operation to broaden its appeal. Unlike the TIM, which readily adapted to this role, a motorised base to power the machine was never developed.

The 'provincial Gibson', as the machine with the revised handle arrangement is sometimes referred to, really represents the last phase of development of the design. The very positive 'clunk' accompanying the selection of fare values was replaced by an arrangement where the selector knob had to be pulled outwards and turned to change fare value. This may have been a cost saving exercise, as the feature needed fewer components and did away with the need for a jig when replacing the fare drum at overhaul. Perhaps too this was another step to making it easier to use mounted on a stand, although it made the rapid selection of fare values somewhat awkward.

Peter Brooks refers to a batch of Gibson machines for Coras Iompair Eireann (C.I.E.) for services in Dundalk in the Republic of Ireland but evidence for their existence is somewhat scant. It is possible they were ex-London disposals.[1]

Despite the circulation of the various demonstrators, sales outside London were a disappointment and the subsequent availability of surplus London equipment no doubt

compounded the problem. It is thought the West Bridgford machines were some of the last built, certainly for the home market, and production had ceased by the end of 1958. Spare parts though continued to be supplied throughout the 1960s, not always to the same quality of the originals.

TEL had effectively become just a brand name within TIM Ltd by that time. As the Gibson and TIM12 were competing for the same customers, no doubt 'product rationalisation' accelerated the former's demise but TIM no doubt recognised the TEL brand was a more palatable alternative to TIM in London Transport circles.

Outside London, none of the provincial UK Gibson users

Opposite page left: The Nyasaland machine illustrated earlier, showing the modified class knob catering for both first and second class travel.

Above: The unique Paddington Telephone Exchange machine.

Right: Tickets from Gibsons supplied to Douglas Corporation on the Isle of Man (top) and (bottom), and the Paddington Telephone Exchange example shown above.

had machines in service after the introduction of decimal currency. As such, they had considerably shorter service lives than most London Gibsons, although judging by the condition of surviving examples, this was largely offset by lower maintenance standards.

Efforts were made to adapt the Gibson for other purposes to increase market share, and a number of 'oddities' arose as a result. One of these was the Gibson A3, which, in spite of the name, was a single price value machine for the likes of swimming baths, recreation grounds and car parks. The deletion of the redundant fare drum gave it a curious unbalanced appearance. There is no evidence that any A3s were sold, another case where TIM and Ultimate had the market largely divided up between them. Certainly no examples have ever come to light.

At least one machine was supplied to the General Post Office for Paddington Telephone Exchange – there may have been others. The purpose of this machine was clearly for use in a canteen or on a mobile vending trolley, as it has values like 'TEA' on the class wheel. The purpose of 'SWE' and 'ET' engravings on the 'fare' selector and class knobs was only readily apparent on inspecting the resulting ticket produced! London Transport also commissioned up to 7 Gibson machines with clear acrylic casing for training and demonstration purposes, of which a few survive including machine 6001 illustrated over. They are to long plate specification and were built to be fully functional and differ only from service machines in that the internal workings are clearly visible.

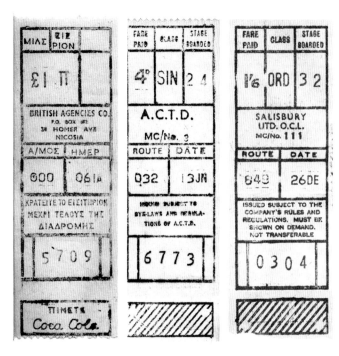

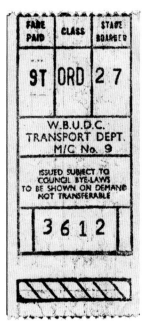

Above left: An example of a provincial Gibson, in this case intended for a Cypriot operator which evidently had no need of the use of stage numbers as an opaque plug has been fitted in lieu of the viewing window in the handle assembly.

Above right: Tickets from this Cypriot machine (left) and similar long plate examples from Accrington and Salisbury, Rhodesia.

Some of the last Gibsons produced for the non-London home market went to West Bridgford. Shown right is the fare drum viewing window and split fare coding that typified these machines and (left), a sample ticket.

The remarkable Gibson variant constructed with acrylic casing so the internal components could be observed in operation for training purposes.

Use on the
London Underground

At various times Gibson machines, like their TIM predecessors, have been in use by London Transport's railways to supplement normal ticketing requirements. Peter Brooks records their use as 'queue busters' where congestion at peak times for station ticket halls was eased by a roving conductor, one such example being at Oxford Circus station. They were also used in this way at secondary station entrances at some of the less busy suburban stations like Roding Valley while in a few applications the machine was mounted at a static booth inside the main barrier for the collection of excess fares, as was the case at Baker Street station.

Ticket evidence supports the existence of 22 Underground Gibsons although there is some circumstantial evidence in support of a conjectural list of 25 as shown. There may have been more - not all were in service at the same time. Their use sometimes gave rise to demarcation problems between booking office staff (salaried status) and ticket collectors which were wages grade. The issue of tickets didn't readily sit well with either Union or management views on what was an appropriate level of responsibility and pay.

M/c No.	Station	Purpose	Comments	Fare range
20032	Watford	excess fares	Short plate with date	Country area range 'B', i.e. 1d, 1½d 2d, 3d, 4d, 5d, 6d, 7d 8d, 9d, 10d, 11d, 1/-, 3/-
22036	Mill Hill East and Croxley at separate times	excess fares		Country area range 'B'
23132	Moor Park	excess fares		Country area range 'B'
24399	Hillingdon	excess fares		Country area range 'B'
25619	Mill Hill East	excess fares		Country area range 'B'
26012	West Finchley	excess fares		Country area range 'B'
26239	Bank	excess fares		Decimal fare range - 1½ 2, 2½, 3, 4, 5, 6, 7, 7½, 8, 9, 10, 11, 12½
27936	Park Royal	excess fares		Country area range 'B'
31218	Boston Manor	excess fares	Short plate with date	Country area range 'B'
32129	Ravenscourt Park	excess fares	Short plate with date	Country area range 'B'
34723	West Acton	excess fares		Country area range 'B'
35314	Ruislip Gardens	excess fares	Short plate with date	Country area range 'B'
35532	Grange Hill	excess fares		Country area range 'B
R1	Bond Street	excess fares	Short plate with date	
R2	Oxford Circus	ordinary ticket issue	Long plate with date	Pre decimal
R3	Roding Valley	ordinary ticket issue	Long plate with date	In LRT Museum, Acton, with high value decimal fares
R4	Marble Arch	excess fares		
R5	?	?		
R6	Leytonstone	excess fares		
R7	Gants Hill	excess fares	Short plate with date	Pre decimal
R8	?	?		
R9	?	?		
R10	Piccadilly Circus	excess fares		
R11	Hammersmith (District & Piccadilly Line)	excess fares		
R52	Baker Street	excess fares (in service November 1951)	Pre-production m/c with replacement type plate	1d, 1½d, 2d, 3d, 4d, 5d, 6½d, 8d, 9d, 10d, 11½d, 1/-, 1/1d, 2/-

The last of these seems to have been a batch of 12 machines for use by the Assistant Operating Manager (Traffic Railways) produced in December 1970. Based on the ticket evidence, these were surplus Country machines, eminently suitable for the task having the benefit of higher fare values and the dating facility, albeit with new type plates fitted.

A proposal was put forward in April 1971 to set aside 200 surplus Gibsons for use in 96 Underground stations most vulnerable to Thames flooding. The self service machines in ticket halls would have been particularly vulnerable in such an eventuality. Quotations were obtained for new type plates and a demonstration machine produced (ticket illustrated right). An increased provision for 300 Gibsons was still being made within the float of surplus machines until early 1981. Thereafter the matter was quietly allowed to lapse, no doubt mindful of the Thames barrier, which was officially opened in 1984, making such contingencies largely unnecessary.

Kerbside conductors

The idea of using a 'kerbside' conductor, taking fares from queuing passengers before they board the bus, was suggested as a means of easing congestion at busy bus stops used by one person operated vehicles. A pilot was proposed for both Barking and East Croydon in 1973 involving 12 numeric Gibsons fitted with a dating facility from redundant Country Area machines. It was necessary to designate the time of ticket issue too and this was done by simply using the fare stage facility; stage 16 for example meant a ticket issued between 16:00 and 16:59 hours.

It is not thought this particular scheme ever got off the ground, but the idea was resurrected for a 6 week trial beginning on November 7th 1977. The location chosen was stop 'F' in Powis Street, Woolwich, used by one person operated bus routes 51 and 96. The method of denoting the hour the ticket was issued by use of the stage number was as previously but this time the route number was set to record the date. A ticket with route wheels set to '712' meant issue on the 7th of December.

It was important to show both the time and the date on the ticket to deter passengers tendering 'kerbside litter' in lieu of valid pre-paid travel. Boarding time was cut from 5 seconds per passenger to 2½ seconds, a good result, but not sufficiently worthwhile to warrant the additional staffing costs.

Circular Tour of London
Another interesting use of Gibson ticket machines was for the Circular Tour of London operated by London Transport's private hire department. Tickets were issued at the start of the tour, which in 1954, according to the publicity poster, ran hourly from 10:00am to 6:00pm in the summer months and started in Buckingham Palace Road, SW.1.

A special type plate was fitted titled 'Circular Tour of London' - the 1967 fares were 2/6d and 5/- for child and adult respectively. The machine was adapted to issue tickets of only these values.

Commemorative tickets
Appendix 4 illustrates the diversity of type plates that were used for special purposes and commemorative events such as overseas tours, a common feature of the 1960's and 1970's, when a Gibson machine would accompany a red London bus promoting Britain and British industry abroad. Generally these were not directly revenue generating operations; the tickets themselves were merely intended as souvenirs and had no face value. Accordingly, the only moveable type featured was to show a serial number and sometimes the date on the ticket.

Left: The queue for a 'Round London Sightseeing Tour' bus captured by photographer Colin Tait in May 1974. Gibson tickets (as per the example illustrated) and publicity material were normally given to passengers before boarding. The use of a closed top DMS class bus was not a particularly inviting proposition! © TfL from the London Transport Museum collection

Gibson Infrastructure

A considerable supporting infrastructure was built around Gibson machines throughout their service lives. Activities included servicing, maintenance and repair: ticket machine transport and distribution: the production of consumables like ticket rolls and waybills and the provision of everyday ancillary items like carrying boxes, webbing, emergency ticket packs etc.

The Ticket Machine Works

Although the Gibson was conceived and built in prototype form at the Stockwell Punch Works, these premises were considered too small for the necessary workshop area to service and repair the expected number of machines once production started and the trickle from Tring became a steady flow. The old LCCT works at Effra Road, Brixton, was the obvious choice but still at that time largely given over to printing punch tickets and in a separate part of the works, the packing and despatch of conductors ticket boxes. This would need to continue while sufficient garages and depots still used punch tickets, so an interim solution had to be found.

Looking to its property portfolio, premises in Bowles Road, off Old Kent Road, were identified as suitable having been previously used as a permanent way depot until closure in 1952 with tram abandonment. The Ticket Machine Works, as it was now known, was relocated there in early November 1953 with the intention of it being a 2 year stay pending a decision on the future of Effra Road. A 12 month lead-in period was deemed necessary to convert Effra Road as a workshop. Bowles Road was considered too small and

Left: An official view of the Effra Road works as it looked in October 1961. After the introduction of Gibson ticket machines, the two main parts of the building, as seen here, naturally leant themselves to the differing tasks of ticket roll production and ticket machine maintenance. © TfL from the London Transport Museum collection

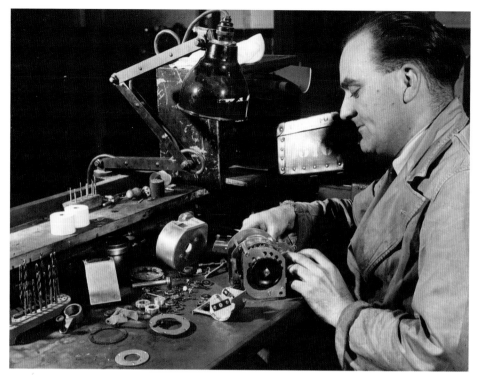

acted upon, as the balance of advantage lay in favour combining ticket roll production and ticket machine maintenance in one place.

The Effra Road premises were duly occupied by the new Ticket Machine Works in January 1956, while building work was still in progress. Conversion costs were estimated to be in the region of £15,000 though this had to be subsequently increased to £23,000 to make provision for extras such as works vans needed to collect and distribute ticket machines from the various garages. The floor too needed to be lowered and office space provided benefiting from natural light. The lack of a suitable 50 cycle power supply for the ticket roll slitting machines was rectified by connection to the Executive's Greenwich Generating Station which powered the trolleybus network and provided secondary capacity for the Underground. Roof panels painted black during the wartime blackout needed replacement and toilet facilities, heavily in favour of female users when Effra Road catered for punch tickets, had to be reconfigured to accommodate, in those pre-equality times, the expected influx of men being engaged in ticket machine maintenance. The final bill for the conversion work was £27,000 (£700,000 in today's terms), nearly twice the initial estimate and the cause for some scrutiny when the matter came before the Executive in October 1956.[1]

expensive to adapt when the full complement of Gibson machines would be in service and an added disadvantage was that it lacked the necessary planning consent to be so used beyond 1960. Another alternative to Effra Road was briefly considered in January 1954, when a proposal to adopt production line methods was floated if both road transport and rail ticketing hardware was maintained at the same works; logically this would be the existing Signal Overhaul Shop at Lillie Bridge. In the event this was not

Above: Craftsman George Simmonds carrying out maintenance work to a Gibson machine at the old Stockwell Punch Works in February 1955.

Right: William Shepheard (left) and Allan Ewins (right) with Setright and Gibson machines. Setright maintenance was required less frequently but machines took longer to work on. A Gibson machine could be stripped and rebuilt within 6 hours in skilled hands. Fare drums were overhauled separately and a stock of ready to fit spares maintained at all times. © TfL from the London Transport Museum collection

The use of Gibson machines at that time was nearing its height and the opportunity was taken to refit the Effra Road works with all new engineering equipment: Fobco Star bench pillar drills, Canning rotary polishers, dust extraction equipment and Boxford lathes as well as new benches and seating. Considerable storage was needed for machines awaiting overhaul and a float was maintained of approximately 10% of the total duty requirement. In later years as the machines aged this was increased to 15% with some of this spare capacity stored in the various garages and depots throughout the network. Gibson light servicing and re-inking was undertaken every 4 months, and every 12 months the machines had a full overhaul involving a complete strip down and replacement of any damaged or defective parts. In later years, a 26 week full overhaul cycle was introduced, reflecting the need for more intervention as parts became worn.

The four works vans would leave Effra Road at night every weekday (every other weekday night from October 1966), loaded with 200 serviced machines for the various Central Area and closest Country Area garages. A fifth went during the day to the outer garages in the Country Area. Each van did the return journey with Gibsons requiring attention. On receipt at the works, each machine would go through the Progress Section where they were divided between those needing normal servicing and those with reported defects and/or needing full overhaul. Preview inspectors would then authorise the work required and allocate an appropriate completion timescale. Weekly output records were kept to measure productivity; an allowance was made for a complete Gibson overhaul of between 5.75 and 6.25 hours.

Ticket machine 'craftsmen', as they were known (staff in this role were never referred to as 'engineers' or 'technicians', a throw back to Punch Works days), would work on each machine from start to finish; 40 operations are reported as required for a full overhaul, 8 for servicing. Machines for overhaul were stripped down and the parts cleaned and carefully checked for wear. The fare drum was overhauled separately from the rest of the machine, both then going to the stores for subsequent reissue; the high degree of parts interchangeability meant on reassembly, machines would rarely be given the same fare drum they began with.

The fibre inking rollers were pressure impregnated with ink and went to an outside contractor in a metal tin for replenishment, or if worn, replacement with a new unit. Ink rollers were good for 80,000 ticket issues. Unlike Gibson machines intended for provincial users, where an aperture was provided in the external casing that allowed ink to be applied to the roller without accessing the internal workings, inking was seen by London Transport as an integral part of the maintenance cycle of the machine. The absence of this aperture is characteristic of all London production Gibsons. It also removed the possibility of machines being reinked 'on the fly' with the likely consequence of over-inking and angry passengers with soiled hands or uniforms ruined by leaks of indelible ink.

Finally, machines ready for reissue were carefully checked and the readings from the 14 individual fare drum counters were added up to ensure they tallied with the total tickets counter. Very high maintenance standards were maintained at all times enabling Gibsons to have long service lives and this is still evident in the condition of many survivors today. In addition to servicing ticket machines, the works also maintained all the vending machines (tea, coffee, cold drinks, snacks, etc.) provided for staff at its various premises.

The opportunity to service Gibson ticket machines in use by Douglas Corporation arose in June 1966 when D.E. Halsall, the Joint Controller of Douglas' Transport Department had occasion to write to D.S. James, the Works Superintendent who had replaced Charles Speller, asking if Effra Road could help. TEL in Cirencester apparently had a 6 month backlog at the time. A.E. Shave, the Chief Supplies Officer, replied to the effect that unfortunately he was unable to assist as the 1962 Transport Act precluded London Transport, in common with other transport undertakings in public ownership, undertaking commercial work for non-nationalised bodies.

At its height, Effra Road employed 114 staff, 76 of them engaged solely on ticket machines: Gibson, Ultimate and Setright SM.B ticket equipment.[2] Later, AFC equipment and Almex machines joined this list. In 1982, 63 people were engaged in ticket machine maintenance of all grades, 8 were needed for ticket roll production, 8 for maintaining vending machines and a further 10 staff were employed in an administrative capacity. At the time, the annual cost of maintaining a Gibson machine was £71 compared to £56 for an Almex Model E, largely reflecting the relative ages involved. [3]

Below: One of the four Harnden slitting and winding machines in operation at Effra Road—behind, the pulp paper reels from Bowaters are stored ready for use.

Right: Ticket rolls were wound onto their cores individually once the bulk reel had been slit to the correct size. Complete rolls then passed down this conveyor to be packed in cartons of 200. © TfL from the London Transport Museum collection

Effra Road survived various productivity studies in the 1980s and in 1985 became part of London Regional Transport's arm's length engineering wing known as Bus Engineering Ltd (BEL). It closed though shortly afterwards and activity relocated to Chiswick, as the building was too large for the dwindling number of mechanical machines in use and needed urgent remedial works included a new roof. In January 1988, BEL was sold to Frontsource Ltd which had earlier acquired many of the engineering establishments belonging to the National Bus Company that had similarly been privatised. Gibson machines continued to be maintained until the last were withdrawn in 1993, despite Frontsource going into receivership in 1989 to be acquired by Bus Engineering Group.

This brought about a move from Chiswick to new premises at Salter Street, Willesden, where Gibson maintenance work continued, albeit on a reduced scale. At about this time George Sawyer retired as manager having been closely involved with the Gibson machine since joining the Punch Works at Stockwell and latterly as Ticket Machine Works Superintendent at Effra Road, taking over from D.S. James in 1981. One of his last tasks was preparation of 150 reconditioned machines for use in Kano, Nigeria and readying surplus machines for sale to the public through the London Transport Museum shop in Covent Garden. This required removal of the 'London Transport' title from the type plate while Gibsons remained in revenue earning service. Rod Lucas succeeded George Sawyer as works manager and his recollections of those times are contained in his excellent book, 'Shades of Green and Red'. [4]

Ticket roll production

One similarity between the Gibson and the TIM machine was that they both used the same size of ticket rolls. Wartime TIM rolls adopted for the early Gibson trials were of notoriously poor quality and 'concertinaring' was the most prominent defect, helped later by the use of better grade paper. Ticket rolls for the TIM machines were supplied by National Cash Registers (NCR) Ltd until January 1953 when the order was split between NCR and British Waxed Wrappings Ltd. External contracts were issued until the end of 1955 for the estimated 17 million rolls per year needed as deliveries of Gibson machines gathered pace.

The last punch tickets were produced at Effra Road in May 1956, thereafter the need for pre-printed tickets was met by Bell Punch Ltd. Work then got underway installing the necessary plant to equip for in-house ticket roll production, most prominently the four large Harnden machines for slitting and winding the paper rolls. Bulk paper mill reels from Bowaters, each 38 inches wide and weighing 3 cwt,

were loaded on to each Harnden machine, the paper was passed over steel rollers, slit to the correct width of 1 7/16th of an inch and then wound on to cardboard cores producing each roll individually in a line of 26. The outside diameter of the roll had to be no greater than 2 inches: any bigger and it wouldn't fit in the ticket roll holder on the machine. Rolls were good for 375 issues in short plate configuration. A green line appeared on the tickets warning the conductor of imminent exhaustion of the paper roll.

Part of the production process required rolls to be pressed to even out any ridges and passed on a conveyor system to the point where they were packed, 200 at a time, into cardboard cartons. On the eve of Effra Road works opening in 1956, the planned-for annual production was to be 9 million ticket rolls, which represented 90% of the Executive's requirements and the equivalent of 3.2 billion individual tickets. Reductions in the number of duties by 1964 meant Effra Road was able to produce all it needed, amounting to 7.75 million rolls annually, enough paper apparently to encircle the earth six times!

The manufacturing process allowed ticket roll cores to be recycled and staff were instructed in 1954 to place used cores in their ticket boxes, although this practice was discontinued in 1961. The passing of partly spent ticket rolls to youthful passengers was frowned upon, as evidenced by criticism in November 1954 by the irate Headmaster of the Picardy Secondary School for Boys, served by trolleybus route 698 from Bexleyheath depot. Any fascination the boys had retaining rolls as transport mementos was quickly overtaken by their suitability as streamers, much to the annoyance of the school caretaker.

Roll cores produced for Gibson machines at Effra Road were dark blue. Ticket rolls were also produced at the works for the magnetic tape Almex A.763 machine which came with a green core, the Almex Model E had a light blue core and the standard Almex Model A a black one when these machines came in to use. Some of the rolls produced were sold to Almex for outside operators, a practice made possible by a change of legislation in 1968. It is not thought Gibson rolls were ever produced at Effra Road for the small number of provincial users of the machine.

Mention has been made of the coloured paper rolls used for Country Area Rover tickets. In his article, Peter Brooks also describes the use of grey rolls for kerbside issue for Wimbledon tennis tournament services and pink rolls, much darker than for those produced for Country buses, for the Woolwich kerbside conductors experiment in 1977.

That same year marked the Queen's Silver Jubilee and to mark the event, 25 Routemasters received a special all-over silver livery and external advertising in accordance with the relevant commercial sponsorship. Special Gibson ticket rolls in pale primrose were produced carrying the sponsor's logo: 494 cartons of 200 rolls and produced to 25 different designs for household names such as Kosset Carpets, Addis Wisdom toothbrushes and Kleenex tissues. Two separate designs were produced for Woolworths; Nat West, although sponsoring a Routemaster, didn't opt for the use of special ticket rolls.

General advertising on ticket rolls would have been a useful source of revenue, as it had been in punch ticket days, but Effra Road lacked the necessary facility to print on the reverse of the paper as it passed on to the core winder. The Silver Jubilee rolls therefore had to be outsourced to NCR.

As late as 1976, a proposal was put forward extending the length of the Gibson type plate to carry sponsored advertising, like the Coca-Cola slogans

Left: Experience from the pre-service trials, and the convening of the research team chaired by Dr Gilks, settled opinion on the best means of carrying the machine on the cross braced style of harness, using webbing similar to that used in car seat belts, to help distribute the weight as evenly as possible.

Right: Although the webbing was designed to engage four attachment lugs on the exterior of the machine, conductors would still adopt variations in how it was carried, as evidenced in this 1956 view with only the uppermost lugs in use. The Gibson was designed to sit high on the chest but some staff preferred a lower position resting on the abdomen. © TfL from the London Transport Museum collection

on some machines for export. It is likely though the costs of producing and fitting new type plates was prohibitive, particularly when bearing in mind the relatively short term nature of some advertising contracts. The closest this idea got to widespread introduction was the sponsorship details of the various commemorative type plates produced for special occasions and tours illustrated in Appendix 4.

Ticket rolls with coloured edges in yellow, brown or green, were used for tickets for the London Circular Tour using an adapted Gibson machine with 2/6d and 5/- fare values and a specially titled type plate. Likewise, Wimbledon Tennis Tournament services used colour edged rolls, as did the Alexandra Palace Rose Show - no doubt other special events as well. When the railway bridge at West Drayton was rebuilt in 1959

severing bus routes passing underneath, passengers had to break their journey and rejoin another bus on the other side. Different colour edged rolls were used each day to ensure only passengers reboarding were entitled to do so. This occurred again in 1962 when Worcester Park railway bridge was closed. The stock of 55,000 coloured edge rolls was deemed surplus to foreseeable needs in November 1963 and some were released for general use giving rise to speculation that these were special issues for Christmas.[5]

By 1971, Gibson ticket roll production at Effra Road was 3.9 million for the Central Area buses and 340,000 for London Country. As late as 1984, over a million Gibson ticket rolls per year were still being produced as well as ticket roll requirements for all Almex machines. Three of the four Harnden machines though mostly lay idle. The works was also responsible for receipt, storage and issue of all the pre-printed tickets in use for road and rail services.

Webbing

Difficulties securely attaching prototype machines to a suitable harness, and concerns about the weight in comparison to punch equipment, prompted London Transport to take the matter of how the machine was to be carried extremely seriously. The Executive's Research and Development Committee considered the matter in July 1950 and resolved to set up an operational research team with the remit "to recommend the most suitable form of harness to be provided for the ticket issuing machines used by the conductors on road service vehicles". As mentioned earlier, this team was chaired by the Assistant Medical Officer, Dr A.W. Gilks, and also consisted of the Joint Commercial Managers, the Operating Manager of Central Road Services and the Chief Development and Research Officer. [6]

Dr Gilks wisely recognised the need to have staff representation on this research team from both Central

Area and Country Area conductors. Effort was also made to reduce the weight of the machine: the pre-production Gibson weighed 4lb 3oz (1.9kg) but with modification, this was reduced to 3lb 15oz (1.8kg).

The research team initially looked at where on the body the Gibson machine should be carried. Dr Gilks commented "it is such a shape and size that it must rest at some point against the ribs, unless (worn) very low down when it would rest entirely against the abdominal wall. If (worn) further to the side, it rests against bony ribs where there is greater risk of injury". He concluded that in any event there was no significant risk of harm by wearing the machine in any position. High on the chest and in a central position was the method adopted and although this was not always comfortable for some staff, it allowed free movement of both hands and removed the risk of the machine striking objects or passengers heads if worn lower or to the side. [7]

Although the original tender from Crawley Ticket Machines was for supply of both harnesses and fibre carrying boxes, both were actually sourced independently. Studies were undertaken with various materials but webbing as opposed to leather straps was adopted, largely to evenly distribute the weight of the machine on the shoulders. Two individual sections of webbing were provided and stitched in the middle to form an 'X' pattern with four anchorage clips and a leather apron to protect the uniform tunic, later made of black synthetic leather. Indeed it was known as 'X type' webbing to distinguish it from the 'Y type' used for the TIM12 which had only three anchorage points. Four loops were provided on the outside casing of the Gibson machine to allow it to be securely held by the webbing.

Records are incomplete but we know Brookhill Productions Ltd won the tender for the supply of webbing for the first batch of 10,000 machines and may have fulfilled subsequent orders.

Carrying boxes

Carrying boxes for Gibson machines were made out of vulcanised fibreboard, the same material used for punch ticket boxes, being light and relatively easy to fabricate into a box shape. Unlike metal boxes though, they were not particularly robust.

The standard Gibson box had a central division and cutaway section that engaged the base of the handle when placed in the box, effectively anchoring it when the lid was closed. A separate section was provided for spare ticket rolls, the pack of emergency tickets and other items according to the conductor's preference. As the original straight sided boxes became worn out, a different style was adopted, slightly taller and narrower with tapered inner edges. Lids were secured with leather straps and a buckle but these had the tendency to break as the leather became worn and cracked.

The outside of boxes had the machine number painted on and often the duty number and garage code as well, depending on where the machine was allocated, although in the Country Area, where duties were interworked, some of this information was usually omitted.

Various firms over the years have been associated with supplying the ticket boxes, perhaps foremost among them the Excelsior Fibre Company of Oldham which also undertook repairs to boxes. The boxes for the initial order of 10,000 machines were supplied at a cost of 15/- each (£20 in today's terms) by Gla-Rev Products Ltd of

Fowler Road, Hainault. The well-known firm of Henry Jew & Co. Ltd. of Birmingham was a supplier in punch days and may also have provided fittings for boxes and possibly webbing too. J.Burns Ltd was another well-known supplier of boxes and, while records are scant on this subject, may also have manufactured boxes for London use.

Typically, a fibre box would last about 15 years so most machines would have got through two or possibly even three boxes in a lifetime. Edges were reinforced with corner gussets and the straps and buckles could be detached and replaced. Austin Miles Ltd were public sector contractors able to source a range of products and it is known that they were engaged at one time with ticket box repairs for London Transport.

Emergency ticket packs

Gibson machines proved reliable in service but in the event of a breakdown, at a limited number of points in central London and from garages en-route, a spare machine could be called upon. A surviving list of collection points from 1959 has eleven identified: Victoria, Aldgate Minories, Liverpool Street station, Golders Green, Kings Cross, Crystal Palace, North Finchley, Elephant & Castle, Craven Park, Wood Green Underground station and Morden Underground station. Ten garages are listed as holding spare machines for emergency use.

Old Bell Punches were also available for the same purpose from a wider number of points and this remained the case until at least 1965. These were for use with the pack of emergency pre-printed tickets supplied in ticket machine boxes although tickets would often be validated by simply being torn in half. A typical emergency tickets pack from 1952 would consist of 200x1d tickets, 100x1½d, 200x2d, 200x3d and 100x5d.

Security arrangements

Keeping a careful tally of machines in service was seen as critical in combating fraud. The clandestine use of a 'second' machine by road staff, in addition to the official one issued for the duty, was one means of making it possible to record takings significantly lower than the actual amount received. The serial numbers of lost or stolen machines were regularly circulated and inspectors would be on the lookout for any tickets turning up in service use that had hitherto been struck off charge. An addendum to staff instructions issued in 1968 warned that the maximum recharge for wilful damage to a machine would be £5 but in all cases where a machine was lost, this was £8.

Chief Inspectors at garages were responsible for undertaking a nightly check of all machines 'on charge' or away for repair. Every two weeks, ticket boxes would be opened and a physical check made of each machine. Any discrepancies had to be immediately reported to the Divisional Superintendent who in turn had to notify the Traffic Audit Office, the Superintendent of the Ticket Machine Works and Head Office.

No comprehensive list of lost machines has come to light but as an illustration of the problem, a total of 15 machines were lost over the preceding 6 months to May 1964 alone and this may not be atypical. This fact alone fuelled the debate as to whether Central Area Gibson machines should issue Red Rover tickets. With a growing number of machines unaccounted for, the potential loss of revenue was obvious were such high value tickets produced by a bogus machine.

Waybills and instructions to conductors

The design of waybills did not markedly change over the years, providing as it did the means to record both opening and closing readings for each duty worked and assist in calculating the cash value of tickets sold. An additional 10 minutes of paid paying in time was allowed reflecting the need for conductors to work out the cash equivalent of each counter reading. This had been the case since LGOC days. Country waybills had provision for the use of Gibson machines over a two day period.

A cash total sheet was completed at duty end and submitted with monies paid in. Reproduced in the appendix is the 'Instructions to Conductors' leaflet that accompanied the machine in its early days, although as stocks of these became exhausted the booklet was not subsequently reprinted so finding an original one now is quite difficult.

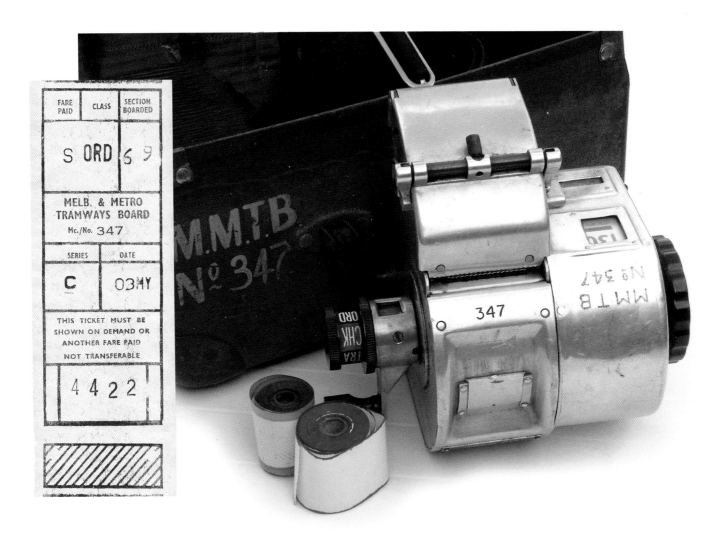

Above: Melbourne & Metropolitan Tramways Board was the largest Gibson user outside London and bought both new machines from TEL (as here) and surplus London Transport equipment as well. In later life these machines were converted to Alpha format, like their London equivalents, but in other respects they remained remarkably unchanged throughout their lives. The absence of the fret between the fare and class values would suggest use originally with the wider style of fare typewheel, which was briefly in vogue in 1955, the likely date of manufacture of this example.

References

Conception

1) Internal audit paper by A.G. Evershed for the Audit Officer entitled 'Comparison between cost of tickets printed at Effra Road and the price paid to the Bell Punch Company' dated 9th March 1948
2) Draft report to the Executive by JHF Benford, Fares and Charges Officer, entitled 'Mechanical Ticket Issuing – Road Services' dated 22nd July 1948
3) Internal audit paper (unattributed) entitled 'Estimated Annual Expenditure in Connection with Tickets' dated 2nd June 1948
4) Report by JP Thomas, Commercial Manager, to the Board's Ticket Committee, entitled 'Ticket Machines' dated 7th December 1936
5) Study entitled 'Speed of Issue Test' undertaken in November 1946 contained in the Report to the Executive by JHF Benford, Fares and Charges Officer, entitled 'Mechanical Ticket Issuing – Road Services' dated 9th August 1948
6) Paper by BH Harbour, Commercial Manager, to the General Managers Traffic Meeting No 32, entitled 'Road Services – Ticket Machines' dated 31st January 1945.
7) Report to the Executive by JHF Benford, Fares and Charges Officer, entitled 'Mechanical Ticket Issuing – Road Services' dated 9th August 1948
8) Internal memorandum from JHF Benford, Fares and Charges Officer to LC Hawkins of the Executive, headed 'TIM – Ticket Issuing Machines Ltd' dated 5th December 1949.
9) Report to the Executive by JHF Benford, Fares and Charges Officer, entitled 'Mechanical Ticket Issuing – Road Services' dated 9th August 1948
10) Memorandum to the Executive from joint Commercial Managers BH Harbour and D McKenna, entitled 'Mechanical Ticket Issue – Road Services' dated 26th September 1950.

Birth

1) Internal memorandum from BHF Benford, LPTB Fares and Charges Officer to AH Grainger, LPTB Solicitor General, entitled 'Ticket Issuing Machines' dated 24th November 1944
2) Article in 'London Bus Magazine', Number 66, Autumn 1988, entitled 'A Forgotten Anniversary' by Peter Brooks, published by the London Omnibus Traction Society, www.lots.org.uk
3) Internal memorandum from AH Grainger, LPTB Solicitor General to BHF Benford, Fares and Charges Officer, entitled 'Ticket Issuing Machines' dated 30th November 1944

4) Internal memorandum from BHF Benford, LPTB Fares and Charges Officer to BH Harbour, Commercial Manager, entitled 'Stockwell Punch Works Ticket Issuing Machine' dated 11th December 1944
5) Internal memorandum from BHF Benford, LPTB Fares and Charges Officer to BH Harbour, Commercial Manager, entitled 'Stockwell Punch Works Ticket Issuing Machine' dated 22nd February 1945
6) Internal memorandum from CG Page, Secretary to the London Passenger Transport Board to TE Thomas, Commercial Manager, entitled 'Ticket Issuing Machine – Provisional Patent 25938/44' dated 26th March 1945
7) 'Heads of Agreement' between Mr G Gibson and CG Page, Secretary to the London Passenger Transport Board, entitled 'LPTB and Mr G Gibson' dated 29th May 1945
8) Internal memorandum from BHF Benford, LPTB Fares and Charges Officer to BH Harbour, Commercial Manager, entitled 'Gibson's Application for Letters Patent' dated 1st December 1944
9) Internal memorandum from PG Gibbins, Divisional Superintendent, Trams & Trolleybuses, Vauxhall to TJ Tilston, Operating Manager, Trams & Trolleybuses, entitled ' "Gibson" Ticket Issuing Machine', dated 24th October 1945
10) Internal memorandum from AH Hawkins, General Manager, Country Buses and Coaches to BH Harbour, Commercial Manager, entitled '"Gibson" Ticket Issuing Machine' dated 16th October 1945
11) Internal memorandum from JB Burnell, Operating Manager, Central Buses to BHF Benford, Fares and Charges Officer, entitled '"Gibson" Ticket Issuing Machine' dated 5th November 1945

Coming of Age

1) Hand written memorandum from George Gibson, Superintendent, Punch Works to BHF Benford, Fares and Charges Officer (untitled) dated 18th April 1946
2) Letter from FJ Cleveland & Co, Bank Chambers, 29 Southampton Buildings, Chancery Lane, London WC2 addressed to the Assistant Secretary, London Passenger Transport Board, entitled 'British Patent Application No. 25938/44 – Ticket Machine – George Gibson' dated 22nd May 1946
3) Report 'Memorandum for the Executive' entitled 'Mechanical Ticket Issue – Road Services' by D McKenna, Commercial Manager dated 20th March 1951 citing the Signal Engineer's examination of the Gibson ticket machine undertaken in 1946

4) Study entitled 'Speed of Issue Test' undertaken in November 1946 contained in the Report to the Executive by JHF Benford, Fares and Charges Officer, entitled 'Mechanical Ticket Issuing – Road Services' dated 9th August 1948

5) Report to the Executive entitled 'Mechanical Ticket Issuing – Road Services' by JHF Benford, Commercial Manager, dated 9th August 1948

6) Internal memorandum entitled 'Mechanical Ticket Issuing Machines – Road Services' from LC Hawkins of the Executive to London Transport Executive Chairman Lord Latham dated 17th April 1950

7) Report 'Memorandum for the Executive' entitled 'Mechanical Ticket Issue – Road Services' by the Joint Commercial Managers dated 26th September 1950

8) Minutes of a meeting held at Reigate chaired by R Postgate 'To Review Progress of the Gibson Machines' dated 28th March 1950

9) Extract from minutes of Informal Road Services Meeting – minute 204/12/49 'Purchase of 1000 TIM Machines' dated 21st December 1949

10) Report entitled 'Ticket Issuing Machines – Reports from the District Superintendents and Conductors on Tests in Service' from the Operating Manager (Central Buses) dated 31st May 1946

11) Internal memorandum entitled 'T.I.M. (Ticket Issuing Machines) Ltd' from JHF Benford, Commercial Manager to LC Hawkins, Office of the Executive dated 5th December 1949

12) Memorandum to the Executive entitled 'Purchase of 1000 Ticket Issuing Machines' by the Chief Technical Planning and Supplies officer dated 21st February 1950

13) 'Heads of Agreement' between Mr G Gibson and CG Page, Secretary to the London Passenger Transport Board, entitled 'LPTB and Mr G Gibson' dated 29th May 1945

14) Letter addressed to the Secretary, London Transport Executive, from David Colville, Managing Director, Crawley Ticket Machines Ltd of New Court, St Swithin's Lane, London, EC4 dated 30th January 1950

15) File Note from D McKenna, Joint Commercial Manager entitled 'Gibson Ticket Machine' containing a summary of a meeting that had taken place on 20th July 1950 between himself, C Speller, Superintendent, Stockwell Punch Words and the directors of Crawley Ticket Machines; D. Colville (Managing Director), GS Mundell and AML Ponsonby

16) Derived from official records and also cited in an article in 'London Bus Magazine', Number 66, Autumn 1988 entitled 'A Forgotten Anniversary' by Peter Brooks, published by the London Omnibus Traction Society, www.lots.org.uk

Adolescence

1) Minute 217/11/50 from the Central Bus Committee meeting of 22nd November 1950 chaired by JB Burnell, Operating Manager, Central Road Services

2) Letter from W Hilton, Purchasing Officer, London Transport Executive dated 4th April 1951 to DR Colville, Managing Director, Crawley Ticket Machines Ltd, headed 'Ticket Issuing Machines' setting out the points of agreement at the meeting held 3rd April 1951 at 55 Broadway concerning the order for 10,000 Gibson ticket machines

3) Letter addressed to D McKenna, Joint Commercial Manager from David Colville, Managing Director, Crawley Ticket Machines Ltd of New Court, St Swithin's Lane, London, EC4 dated 12th April 1951

4) Minutes of Informal Supplies Meeting No 175, 16th March 1954 – item 88/3/54 'Gibson Ticket Issuing Machines: 'Rise and Fall' Claim'

5) Letter addressed to D McKenna, Joint Commercial Manager from David Colville, Managing Director, Ticket Equipment Ltd of New Court, St Swithin's Lane, London, EC4 dated 24th April 1953

6) Internal memorandum from BH Harbour, Operating Manager Country Buses and Coaches to JB Burnell, Operating Manager, Central Road Services, entitled 'Gibson Ticket Issuing Machine' dated 21st March 1951

7) Minute 228/5/54 of the Executive Conference, memorandum submitted by JB Burnell, Operating Manager Central Road Services, BH Harbour, Operating Manager Country Buses and Coaches, D McKenna, Joint Commercial Manager, EC Ottaway, the Chief Supplies Officer, concerning authority to order a further 7000 Gibson ticket machines in advance of final approval for a Special Expenditure Request

Maturity

1) Internal memorandum concerning draft Memorandum to the Executive from EC Ottaway, Chief Supplies Officer to CW Speller, Superintendent, Ticket Machine Works, entitled 'Gibson Ticket Machine' dated 28th October 1955

2) Memorandum to the Executive from EC Ottaway, Chief Supplies Officer, entitled 'Modification of Gibson Ticket Machines' dated 15th December 1956

3) Memorandum for the Executive, paper entitled 'Green Rover Tickets' from Operating Manager (Central Road Services), Operating Manager (Country Buses and Coaches), Operating Manager (Railways) and Commercial Manager dated 8th December 1958

4) Office of the Assistant Chief Mechanical Engineer (Workshops) Minutes of the Effra Road Works Meeting No. 225, 5th August 1975

5) Memorandum to the Executive from Chief Operating Manager (Buses), Chief Supplies Officer and Chief Financial Officer, entitled 'Decimalisation – Conversion of Gibson Bus Ticket Issuing Machines' dated 19th August 1970

6) Office of the Director of Mechanical Engineering (Workshops and Plant) Minutes of the Ticket Machine Works (Buses) Meeting No. 178, 23rd February 1971

7) Memorandum to the Chief Business Planning Officer from the Chief Public Relations Officer, entitled 'Ticket Machines – Alpha Codes' dated 2nd December 1977

8) Memorandum for the Executive, paper entitled 'Mechanisation of Ticket Issue on Road Services' from Operating Manager (Central Road Services), Operating Manager (Country Buses and Coaches), Chief Financial Officer, Commercial Officer, Chief Supplies Officer dated 2nd April 1957

9) Extract of Minute 174/4/59 - Supplies Meeting No.284, held on 29th April 1959, chaired by EC Ottaway, Chief Supplies Officer, entitled 'Authority to Withdraw Redundant Assets'.

The Search for a Replacement

1) Memorandum for the Executive, paper entitled 'Ticket Issuing System - Road Services' from Chief Supplies and Services Officer, Chief Financial Officer, Commercial Manager, Chief Establishment Officer, Operating Manager (Central Road Services), Operating Manager (Country Buses and Coaches), dated 6th April 1959

2) Memorandum to LC Hawkins, Office of the Executive from EC Ottaway, Chief Supplies & Services Officer, entitled 'Almex Ticket Machine' dated 30th April 1959

3) Extract from Traffic Committee Meeting, chaired by Mr Frank Pick, minute 2991 entitled 'Railways – Ticket Issuing Machines' memorandum from JP Thomas, Commercial Manager dated 29th June 1938

4) Extract from the Minutes of the London Transport Board, minute 1391 entitled 'Provision of 450 Road Services Ticket Issuing Machines and Associated Magnetic Tape Reading Equipment for Extended Trial Purposes' from the Chief Mechanical Engineer (road Services), the Chief Operating Manager (Central Buses), the Operating Manager (Country Buses and Coaches), the Management Services Officer and the Chief Supplies Officer dated 24th July 1968

5) Memorandum for the Executive Conference, report entitled 'Manual Ticket Issuing Machines for 1971 Vehicle Replacement Programme' from Chief Operating Manager (Buses), Chief Supplies Officer, Chief Financial Officer dated 7th August 1970

6) Memorandum from DS James, Superintendent Ticket Machine Works, Effra Road to the Staff Superintendent (Buses), entitled 'Experimental Almex Machines – Palmers Green' dated 5th July 1974

7) Memorandum for the Investment Committee, paper entitled 'Portable Ticket Machines' from Chief Operating Manager (Buses), Chief Supplies Officer and the Chief Financial Officer dated 25th August 1977

8) Memorandum to the Executive entitled 'Portable Ticket Machines' from Operating Manager (Buses), Chief Supplies Officer and the Chief Financial Officer dated 1st September 1978

9) Memorandum to the Board of London Buses Ltd, report entitled 'Replacement of Drivers' Ticket Machines and the Associated Accounting System', from the Operations Director and Finance Director, dated 14th March 1986

10) Memorandum to the Management Meeting of London Buses Ltd entitled 'Development of Portable Electronic Ticket Machine' from the Operations Director, London Buses Ltd dated 14th March 1991

Provincial Gibsons

1) Article in 'London Bus Magazine', Number 66, Autumn 1988, entitled 'A Forgotten Anniversary' by Peter Brooks, published by the London Omnibus Traction Society, www.lots.org.uk

2) List provided courtesy of David Harman, Transport Ticket Society

Gibson Infrastructure

1) Memorandum for the Executive, paper entitled 'Conversion of Premises at Effra Road for Use as a Ticket Machine Works' from Chief Civil Engineer, Architect and Chief Supplies Officer, dated 5th October 1956.

2) London Transport Magazine (London Transport's in house staff magazine), article entitled 'Keeping 16,000 Road Ticket Machines Turning Smoothly' September 1964 issue.

3) Internal departmental study entitled 'Summary of an Investigation into the Effra Road Ticket Machine Works' from the Central Productivity Unit dated 19th April 1982.

4) Book 'Shades of Green And Red' by Rod Lucas published by Capital Transport Publishing, PO Box 250, Harrow, HA3 5ZH, 2006.

5) Journal of the Transport Ticket Society, January 1964, article entitled 'London News' published by the Transport Ticket Society, www.transport-ticket.org.uk

6) Extract of the Minutes of Meeting 36 of the Research and Development Committee No.36 held 14th July 1950.

7) Memorandum from Dr AW Gilks, Assistant Medical Officer to D McKenna, Commercial Manager entitled 'Gibson Ticket Machine' dated 31st March 1951

Appendix 1:
Conversion Dates by Garage/Depot

London Transport Central Road Services Gibson conversion dates

Date of introduction	Garage/ depot	No of machines (correct 27/8/52)	Routes (correct 27/8/52)
16/08/1953	Isleworth	58	657
16/08/1953	Fulwell	228	601, 602, 603, 604, 605, 667
01/11/1953	Southall	257	55, 83, 92, 97, 105, 120, 211
15/11/1953	Hanwell	228	607, 655
06/12/1953	Alperton	183	18, 79, 83, 95, 187
10/01/1954	Stonebridge	207	626, 628, 660, 662, 664, 666
14/02/1954	Willesden	318	6, 8, 18, 46, 52, 112, 291
28/02/1954	Colindale	84	645, 664, 666
07/03/1954	Hendon	217	13, 83, 113, 142, 183
14/03/1954	Carshalton	75	654
28/03/1954	Finchley	185	521, 609, 621, 645, 660
11/04/1954	Potters Bar	148	29, 84, 107, 207
02/05/1954	Highgate	352	513, 517, 611, 613, 615, 617, 627, 639, 653
16/05/1954	Barking	300	9, 23, 62, 87, 145, 148, 174, 175, 295
20/06/1954	Upton Park	440	15, 23, 40, 86, 100, 101, 129, 145, 175
27/06/1954	Hornchurch	242	66, 86, 103, 123, 165, 174, 175, 238, 246, 247, 248, 249, 250, 252
27/06/1954	Seven Kings	186	25, 26, 86, 139, 145, 147, 148, 150, 298
11/07/1954	Romford	158*	Not listed
11/07/1954	Clay Hall	138	8, 10, 25, 26, 60
18/07/1954	Abbey Wood	43	161, 177, 182, 186
18/07/1954	Bexley	167	696, 698
15/08/1954	Plumstead	203	53, 99, 122, 153, 161, 186
17/10/1954	Lea Bridge	46	555, 581
17/10/1954	Clapton	145	555, 581, 677
31/10/1954	New Cross	189	21, 163, 177, 182, 186
28/11/1954	Brixton	173	50, 57, 95, 109, 133, 287
05/12/1954	Peckham	253	12, 21, 36, 70, 78, 173, 177, 182, 186, 188, 286
12/12/1954	Rye Lane	204	1, 12, 69, 149, 163, 172, 179, 285
09/01/1955	Wandsworth	162	28, 44, 91, 168, 170, 288
16/01/1955	Walworth	188	36, 77, 176, 184, 185
23/01/1955	Thornton Heath	106	59, 109, 190
30/01/1955	Clapham	265	45, 50, 104, 137, 155, 168, 169, 181, 189, 287
06/02/1955	Stockwell	80	88, 171, 178
13/03/1955	Croydon	331	12, 59, 64, 68, 115, 130, 133, 159, 166, 197, 234
20/03/1955	Old Kent Road	206	4, 17, 21
17/04/1955	Sidcup	234	21, 51, 132, 161, 228, 229, 241

Date of introduction	Garage/depot	No of machines (correct 27/8/52)	Routes (correct 27/8/52)
24/04/1955	Edmonton	271	627, 649, 659, 679
24/04/1955	Enfield	258	102, 107, 121, 128, 135, 144, 205, 242, 243
10/07/1955	Tottenham	337	34, 61, 67, 73, 76, 104, 144, 236, 290
10/07/1955	Loughton	108	20, 38, 167, 254
14/08/1955	Walthamstow	204	557, 623, 625, 685, 697, 699
28/08/1955	Leyton	370	10, 35, 38, 106, 144, 236, 296
04/09/1955	Stamford Hill	139	543, 643, 647, 649, 683
18/09/1955	Hackney	237	6, 22, 30, 106
25/09/1955	Dalston	315	9, 11, 47, 78, 106, 208
16/10/1955	West Green	176	29, 144, 233
30/10/1955	Turnham Green	180	55, 65, 91, 265
18/11/1956	Riverside	193	11, 17, 27, 71, 72, 88, 91, 289, 297
18/11/1956	Hammersmith	171	626, 628, 630
09/12/1956	Shepherds Bush	84	12, 105
09/12/1956	Kingston	114	152, 215, 216, 218, 219
13/01/1957	Norbiton	124	65, 131, 201, 206, 213, 216, 264, 265
13/01/1957	Twickenham	134	27, 71, 90, 111
27/01/1957	Hounslow	237	33, 81, 98, 110, 111, 116, 117, 162, 203, 237
10/02/1957	Edgware	141	140, 141, 142, 240
24/02/1957	Chalk Farm	227	3, 24, 27, 31, 39, 68, 74, 196
17/03/1957	Holloway	377	4, 14, 19, 27, 43, 58, 134, 143, 171, 172, 196, 292
31/03/1957	Muswell Hill	215	43, 125, 210, 212, 244, 251
07/04/1957	Wood Green	187	625, 627, 629, 641
28/04/1957	Palmers Green	148	29, 34, 84, 102, 112
12/05/1957	Middle Row	200	7, 15, 28, 72, 187
19/05/1957	Harrow Weald	216	114, 140, 158, 209, 221, 230
16/06/1957	Uxbridge	137	98, 204, 220, 222, 223, 224, 225
30/06/1957	Streatham	158	49, 59, 118, 133, 159
30/06/1957	Norwood	158	2, 3, 68, 195
14/07/1957	Elmers End	183	12, 54, 75, 194
11/08/1957	Catford	435	1, 47, 54, 75, 89, 94, 124, 160, 180, 186
08/09/1957	Athol Street	134	56, 82, 108
29/09/1957	Bow	175	661, 663, 695
05/10/1957	West Ham	319	565, 567, 665, 669, 685, 687, 689, 690, 697, 699
05/10/1957	Poplar	159	565, 567, 569, 665
13/10/1957	Ilford	90	691, 693, 695
13/10/1957	Forest Gate	257	25, 66, 96, 145, 147
27/10/1957	Mortlake	170	9, 33, 71, 73
10/11/1957	Chelverton Road	184	28, 30, 37
17/11/1957	Bromley	237	47, 61, 94, 119, 126, 138, 146, 227
24/11/1957	Putney Bridge	216	14, 74, 85, 93, 96
01/12/1957	Sutton	303	80, 93, 115, 151, 156, 164, 213
01/12/1957	Battersea	186*	Not listed
01/12/1957	Merton	459	32, 49, 77, 88, 93, 118, 127, 152, 156, 157, 200

Date of introduction	Garage/ depot	No of machines (correct 27/8/52)	Routes (correct 27/8/52)
09/08/1959	Victoria	TIM	10, 24, 39, 52, 77, 134, 137
16/08/1959	Camberwell	TIM	4, 35, 40, 42, 48, 59, 77, 137, 196
23/08/1959	Cricklewood	TIM	1, 2, 13, 16, 60, 112, 142, 226, 240, 294

London Transport Country Buses Gibson conversion dates

Date of introduction	Garage/ depot	No of machines (correct 27/8/52)	Routes (correct 27/8/52)
(before 12/53)	Garston	111	301, 309, 318, 321, 336, 347, 351, 361
(before 10/54)	Wycombe	52	326, 362, 363, 366, 455, 71
14/03/1954	Watford	96	306, 311, 312, 335, 345, 346, 385
09/05/1954	Amersham	87	305, 309, 336, 348, 397, 353, 359, 362, 373, 398, 394, 703, 709, 710
09/05/1954	Hemel Hempstead	83	301, 302, 307, 314, 316, 317, 322, 337, 377, 708
09/05/1954	Tring	18	301, 352, 387, 706, 707
05/09/1954	Northfleet	120	450, 451, 490, 454, 480, 487, 488, 489, 495, 496, 497, 498, 701, 702
03/10/1954	Dartford	45	401, 423, 467, 491, 486
31/10/1954	Dunton Green	63	402, 403, 404, 413, 421, 431, 454, 471, 704, 705
31/10/1954	Swanley	54	401, 423, 477, 478, 479, 703
12/12/1954	Hertford	124	308, 384, 399, 310, 327, 329, 330, 341, 331, 333, 342, 350, 372, 386, 388, 389, 390, 395, 715
24/04/1955	Epping	36	308, 384, 399, 339, 381, 393, 396, 718, 720
14/08/1955	Windsor	121	335, 407, 417, 441, 442, 444, 445, 446, 457, 458, 459, 474, 484, 704, 705, 718
09/10/1955	Addlestone	68	420, 427, 437, 456, 435, 462, 436, 461, 463, 716, 717
09/10/1955	Staines	47	441, 460, 446, 469, 701, 702
09/12/1956	Guildford	46	408, 415, 425, 432, 436, 448, 463, 715
06/01/1957	Hitchin	15	308, 384, 399, 364, 383, 390, 716
06/01/1957	St. Albans	111	304, 313, 325, 330, 341, 338, 358, 343, 354, 355, 365, 391, 369, 382, 712, 713
06/01/1957	Stevenage	10	Garage opened 1955
07/04/1957	Hatfield	44	303, 330, 341, 340, 392, 717
07/04/1957	Luton	32	321, 356, 376, 360, 364, 714
19/05/1957	Chelsham	65	403, 408, 470, 453, 464, 465, 485, 706, 707
21/07/1957	East Grinstead	30	409, 411, 424, 428, 434, 473, 494, 708
21/07/1957	Godstone	74	409, 410, 411, 709
18/08/1957	Grays	126	315, 328, 323, 349, 380, 370, 371, 374, 375, 723
20/10/1957	Leatherhead	137	406, 408, 470, 416, 418, 419, 422, 435, 462, 468
17/11/1957	Crawley	37	405, 424, 426, 434, 473, 438, 710
24/11/1957	Dorking	32	412, 414, 425, 429, 439, 433, 449, 712, 713, 714
24/11/1957	Reigate	90	405, 406, 409, 411, 414, 429, 439, 430, 440, 447, 711

* Correct at 6/3/195

Appendix 2:
Collecting and Care

Collecting Gibson machines

It is perhaps surprising so many Gibson machines have survived the rigours of service life and are still extant today. This is largely due to the marketing of machines by the London Transport Museum Shop in Covent Garden which offered redundant Gibsons for sale in the 1990s onwards, often with the 'London Transport' title, and sometimes the machine number too, removed from the print plate to prevent fraudulent use. Often they were given a modest overhaul, and were at the very least checked over to ensure those offered for sale were among the better survivors and worked reliably.

Values have fluctuated over the years, but representing the base line is an Alpha machine which, given its relative abundance, should be sourced with the correct box, webbing and a few spare rolls. A small premium is expected for machines in above average condition that print a clear ticket which is properly titled 'LONDON TRANSPORT' and have a carrying box with a matching machine number. 'Numeric' decimalised machines attract marginally higher prices due to scarcity value.

Ascending the rarity ladder, next are the Country Area machines, mostly pre-decimalised although occasionally decimalised machines come to light with the tell-tale 'split fare' strip and 'd' ground off the fare print wheel penny values. Such machines were never officially offered for sale and one wonders sometimes where they originate, although in latter days London Country had no use for them and many were no doubt obtained as souvenirs by road staff.

Left: A 1993 poster illustrating the availability of surplus Gibson machines through the London Transport Museum Shop.

Opposite page top: The Lone Star company produced this working toy Gibson which printed the fare value on an otherwise pre-printed ticket (photograph courtesy of Vectis Auctions Ltd).

care needs to be taken to establish beforehand the very real costs of carriage and import duties.

Assessing the condition of a potential purchase is critical. Unless they are very rare, be wary of machines with heavily dented bodywork which may indicate the machine has been dropped at some stage in the past. The alignment of the three bearings that allow the machine to freely rotate is determined by the two 'B' shaped alloy plates that form both sides of the print drum. Any distortion in this alignment will mean the mechanism will not turn smoothly, which is characteristic of a machine in good order. The condition of these bearings is important too and although robust, they can become clogged with road dirt and seize. Turning the handle should be effortless; any significant resistance will indicate problems and a machine unduly stiff or grating as it rotates should be avoided.

The Gibson's principal fault lies in the arrangement of the print wheels that produce the four-digit serial number that appears on the printed ticket. These are incremented by one at each handle revolution and any resistance felt when the handle is at the '8 o'clock' position, with the machine held upright, means potential problems ahead. The arbour for these wheels within the print drum is made of phosphor bronze which reacts with the mineral based inks used when the machines were in service, producing a greenish deposit. This prevents these wheels rotating freely, with the result often that the machine jams on the serial number overthrow from tens to hundreds or hundreds to thousands. A jammed machine with this problem typically has the total tickets counter ending in 99 or 999, when three or four serial number print wheels are trying to be turned to produce the next sequential number by a relatively inconsequential pin that rotates as the handle is turned. Applying force invariably breaks the pin or a drive gear. The machine will then work freely but with no subsequent progression of the ticket serial number.

Considerably rarer still are genuine pre-decimalised Central Area machines which are highly prized and expect to pay probably upwards of twice the going rate for an Alpha machine.

A handful of pre-production Gibsons survive with private collectors and one, machine no 51, is in the Acton museum reserve collection. Some of these survivors were brought out of retirement briefly in 1972 for use on Prince Marshall's vintage route 100 in London using the preserved Tilling ST, later to be supplanted by punch tickets, an ironic twist really given the norm had always been a Gibson machine replacing a punch!

Understandably, these are rare and highly sought after, as are genuine London Gibsons to long plate specification. When one of the latter came up for auction some years back it sold for a 5 figure sum, so only those with long pockets should aspire to finding one.

Provincial Gibsons and machines for non-transport applications are certainly rare and highly collectable and, as such, command premium prices on those rare occasions one becomes available. Those most frequently encountered, and therefore least valuable, are from Douglas Corporation which were sold through an intermediary to enthusiasts following an advertisement placed in 'Buses' magazine in the early 1970s. Machines from the Melbourne Metropolitan Tramways Board appear occasionally on internet auction sites. If you are purchasing one from Australia, however,

Right: Gibson printed matter is collectable, in this case for the curious fixed value A3 machine.

Fortunately, providing no force is applied, the problem can be corrected by overhaul which involves stripping the print drum, cleaning the affected parts and reassembly. This needs to be undertaken by someone experienced in how the machine works as the necessary phasing of the various drive gears within the print drum on reassembly is beyond the scope of this publication.

Other faults occasionally encountered are ticket issue overrun where the handle continues to turn even through the release button is not depressed. This is due to a sticking or damaged release catch return and correction requires removal of the fare drum. Replacement requires a special jig so this is not a job for the inexperienced.

'Skidding' in the printing of tickets is quite common, as evidenced by sections of the type appearing compressed. This is caused by the paper being allowed to slip in relation to the typeface as it is ejected. Sometimes this can be due to ridges in the ticket roll that prevent it freely turning as tickets are issued. A simple solution is to remove the ticket roll and tap it on a smooth hard surface to remove the undulations. Another cause is too little or too much pressure applied by the rubber contact roller housed in the ticket spool case lid as it comes into contact with the type plate. This is not something that can be readily adjusted. The root problem is often wear in the spool case lid arbour bearings or hardening of the rubber roller. Very gently scouring the print plate with medium coarseness emery paper as the plate passes through the rectangular aperture by turning the handle (ticket spool lid open) can give the plate sufficient traction to resolve the problem but as these plates are likely to be

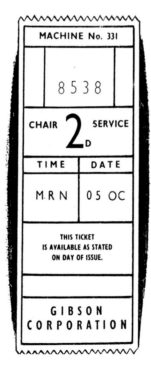

MACHINE No. 331

8538

CHAIR **2**D SERVICE

TIME	DATE
M.R.N	05 OC

THIS TICKET
IS AVAILABLE AS STATED
ON DAY OF ISSUE.

GIBSON
CORPORATION

already heavily worn, care should be taken not to unduly degrade it.

Print impression will also suffer over time, either from the standpoint of the condition of the fibre ink roller, the level of wear of the typeface or the condition of the aforementioned rubber roller. The matter of ink is dealt with below but general wear of the components in the machine is not correctable as replacement parts are generally unavailable and print quality was often problematic even while the machines were in London service.

One feature of typeface wear is that the 'ORD' class value in particular is apt to disappear on printed tickets, as it accounts for the overwhelming majority of issues while in service. As a result the print wheel facet presenting this value gets disproportionately worn.

Care

A machine in good operating condition or one that has been overhauled, will have plenty of life still in it and regular light use will help prevent some of the problems already described.

Particular attention should be paid to storage as damp conditions such as cellars or garages will allow the machine to quickly deteriorate. Tell tale signs of inadequate storage are surface rust on external steel parts such as the webbing clips or screw heads. In extreme cases, the class and stage number arbours become fused due to internal corrosion. Signs of this are the stage number knob and class knob not being able to be turned independently from each other. This fault can only be corrected by stripping down the print drum and separating the seized arbours.

Having last been used in service over a quarter of a century ago, nearly all machines now print faded tickets due to depletion or drying of the ink reservoir in the fibre roller. The ink used was an oil based mineral ink—if you are tempted to open the machine in an effort to reink it, do not use the water soluble inks for use in stamp pads sold by craft shops. It will quickly dry and not only ruin the fibre roller but may also run into the machine where it will set, causing moving parts to seize.

Unfortunately the correct type of ink is not now available and instead I recommend applying a little white spirit to the fibre roller which may temporarily revive ink production sufficient to produce a few tickets but, even if not, you are secure in the knowledge no damage is being done.

If you open the machine, don't be tempted to apply lubricant. I have found to my cost in the past that 3in1 oil makes a very effective adhesive over the passage of time. Liberally dousing the internal parts of your machine in the mistaken belief it will be of benefit will unfortunately render it inoperable in the longer term. The principal movement within your Gibson is carried on the three ball-race bearings that require no lubrication and other components can only effectively be given a light greasing on reassembly after a strip down.

External casing does look very presentable when polished and gentle buffing with a soft dry cloth is all that is needed. Avoid using steel wool as it will scratch the softer alloys used in the machine's construction and care should be taken using Duraglit or the like as the polish tends to run inside the fare drum cover counter windows, fogging them.

Removing the outer casing

For those so inclined, it is relatively easy to remove the outer casing.

1. Locate the single screw securing the locking cap to the fare selector and remove. If the screw is the 'blind head' type you will need to carefully cut or drill a slot in the top to allow a conventional screwdriver to gain purchase on the screw head which undoes anti-clockwise in the conventional manner. Care needs to be taken not to mark the cap itself. An alternative method if you have a square point awl, is to drill a 2—2.5mm hole dead centre in the end of the blind screw and push the point of the awl into the hole and turn anti-clockwise.

2. The end cap can then be pulled off exposing the fare selector knob sitting on its square section spline. The knob itself will need gently levering off with a broad bladed screwdriver, taking care to avoid damaging the fare drum casing.

3. This exposes the two screws sitting in brass cups that secure the fare drum cover. Removing these will allow the fare drum cover itself to be pulled off with a wiggling motion as the square lug on the inside of the cover can foul the fare drum.

3)   3)

4. In a similar manner to the fare selector end cap screw, remove the two screws securing the backplate.

5. (Opposite page) The slotted end to the front cover locking bar is exposed on removal of the fare drum cover. Undo the bar by inserting a small screwdriver and turning anti-clockwise and pull the bar out slightly. There is insufficient clearance to remove the bar completely so instead remove the cover with the loosened bar still in situ. Shown opposite is the bar in place but the cover removed to assist identification.

6. (Opposite page) To replace the front cover, insert the locking bar as shown with the slotted end left. The threaded end of the bar shouid be retained by a finger as the bar and front cover are replaced. The slotted end of this bar needs to be inserted into the small hole as the cover is pushed into place.

Reassembly of the rest of the machine is straightforward and in reverse order. The fare selector knob may need a paper gasket so it sits firmly on the square section spline. A thin strip of ticket roll folded double and laid over the end of the spline as the knob is replaced will suffice.

Specialist advice

The lack of success of the marque outside London meant that no independent maintenance and repair specialists became established in the way they did for the Setright SM.B. Accordingly, it is now very difficult to source specialist knowledge and spare parts for Gibsons, although anyone with a modicum of skill, large reserves of patience and suitable machines to act as guinea pigs, can master the mechanism's intricacies in time.

My father's exploded diagram on page 8 gave me a good understanding of the arrangement of the various internal parts but repeated trial and error has been the method of gaining insight and understanding of the machine's foibles and faults. The majority of machines I have encountered requiring attention merely want overhaul but this involves stripping the machine down fully and rebuilding it having removed the accumulation of dried ink, road dirt and paper dust that have accumulated over many years.

Where parts are required, a degree of invention and ingenuity is called for. Very small quantities of new 'old stock' parts have become available in the past, some hailing many years ago from the Isle of Man, supplemented by a handful of London sourced parts, some of which came from internet auction sites.

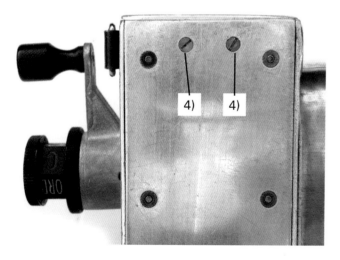

4)   4)

But the main means of obtaining parts comes though from the continued cannibalisation of sub-standard machines. It has also been possible to have remanufactured, or to make myself in the home workshop, some of the components that commonly get broken or continually wear out. New handles and fare selection knobs fall into the first category and are readily available. I have also made replacement rubber contact rollers from medical grade rubber tube which is bonded to a steel arbour providing a like for like replacement of the original. The rubber is supple and improves the print quality of a machine where the original roller has hardened.

Ticket rolls have also been remanufactured for use by the London Bus Preservation Trust but these are not necessarily available to private individuals, although sundry rolls sometimes appear on internet auction sites. Ticket rolls intended for TIM machines will fit the Gibson.

Ink supplies are now exhausted and in spite of attempts to identify a suitable modern equivalent of the original solvent based inks, sadly the technology has moved on and nothing has yet come to light.

New webbing has been remanufactured in recent years and, while not identical to the original, provides adequate support if the machine is to be carried. Internet auction sites are the best place to look.

Local leather workshops can be a useful source of help in repairs to the fibre carrying boxes. In particular the securing strap and buckle, which is apt to snap, are commonplace items in saddlery and other leather goods.

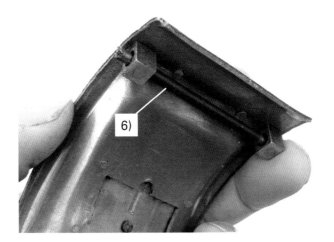

The author welcomes e-mail enquiries about rare or unusual Gibsons and will endeavour to assist readers with queries on repairs or servicing:

ticketronic@btinternet.com

Appendix 3:
Instructions to Conductors

LONDON TRANSPORT EXECUTIVE

Department of the Operating Manager (Central Road Services)

GIBSON TICKET MACHINES

INSTRUCTIONS

TO

CONDUCTORS

INTRODUCTION

1. The Gibson machine is simple to operate and is of robust construction. It is a valuable piece of mechanism, and conductors must at all times exercise care when handling it, particularly when it is being carried in the container, which must at such times be fastened with the strap. In no circumstances should the machine be placed on a seat in a moving vehicle, as a fall to the floor could result in considerable damage to the machine. Conductors are instructed that, whilst in possession of the machine, they are responsible for it and must take every precaution against loss, theft or damage.

DESCRIPTION OF MACHINE

2. The machine prints tickets from a roll of plain paper, and will record on separate counters the number of tickets issued at each of fourteen fare values. These counters are visible through a window at the top of the machine. Adjacent to this window is the counter which records the total number of tickets printed by the machine. This total figure is the number printed on the ticket last issued.

3. Each ticket bears the following details :—
   - (a) Fare paid
   - (b) Class of ticket
   - (c) Number of fare stage boarded
   - (d) Route number
   - (e) Machine number
   - (f) Serial number

Fare setting

4. The ticket value required is obtained by rotating the large wheel (fare change knob) at the left hand side of the machine, until the appropriate value appears in the window at the top of the machine. This wheel may be rotated in either direction.

Fare stage setting

5. To set the stage number, the large inner wheel (stage knob) on the right hand side of the machine must be turned until the required number appears in the small window. This wheel also may be rotated in either direction. The range covered is 01-99.

Class setting

6. The class of ticket required is set by rotating the small outer wheel (class knob) on the right hand side of the machine until the abbreviation for the class required appears on the top of the six-sided wheel. The abbreviations are as follows :—

Ordinary single ticket	ORD
Child single ticket	C
Tickets issued in combination	COM
Early morning single ticket	EMS

Note.—The codes X and C/M are not allocated at present.

Ticket roll

7. The ticket roll is contained under the spool case lid at the top of the machine. To insert a ticket roll, the small fastener on the lid must first be levered upwards with the thumb to allow the lid to be opened. The roll is fitted by pushing it (with the loose end of the roll at the bottom) between the two spring loaded balls, care being taken to ensure that the balls fall into the holes at either end of the cardboard core of the ticket roll, and that the roll rotates freely. The paper must then be adjusted so that it just protrudes from the machine when the lid is closed. Before operating the machine it is essential that the fastener is pressed down to secure the lid, otherwise the pressure required to produce a ticket will not be applied.

8. When a thin green line appears down the centre of the ticket it indicates that the paper has been nearly used up, and that only three more tickets can be issued.

9. The above procedure should be followed when renewing the paper roll. The empty core of the used roll is removed by simply pulling it outwards from the machine.

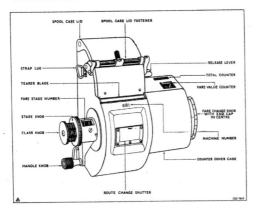

PROCEDURE AT START OF DUTY

10. Having collected the ticket machine in its container from the Output Office, proceed at follows :—

    (a) Check the machine number with that shown on the cash total sheet.

    (b) **On first day.**—Check each individual fare value counter number and the total counter number against those shown on the cash total sheet.
    On second day.—Check each individual fare value counter number and the total counter number against the closing numbers for the first day shown on the cash total sheet.
    Any discrepancy disclosed by the above checks must be reported immediately to the Depot Inspector on duty.

    (c) Ensure that sufficient spare ticket rolls, together with a sealed pack containing emergency tickets and a cash total sheet for use in the event of machine breakdown are available in the machine container.

    (d) Set the fare stage knob to the appropriate position.

    (e) Enter each individual fare value counter number and the total counter number in the appropriate positions in the 1st journey column on the reverse side of the cash total sheet.

PROCEDURE IN SERVICE

Issue of ticket

11. Having set the machine to requirements, as described in paragraphs 4, 5 and 6, a ticket is issued by rotating the handle on the right hand side of the machine one complete turn in a clockwise direction. Before this handle can be turned, the release lever, which is located on the right hand side of the fare value window, must be pressed downwards to release the handle, but once the handle has started to rotate, the pressure on the release lever **must be removed.** This operation of the release lever must be followed between each revolution of the operating handle.

12. The ticket will emerge at the front of the machine and must be torn off by an upwards and sideways movement. If this movement is not employed, the following ticket may "concertina" inside the spool case lid with the result that tickets will not emerge.

13. The attention of conductors is particularly drawn to the fact that each time the handle is started on a revolution, an issue to the value at which the machine is set will be recorded **whether a ticket is printed or not.**

14. 3d and 4d. tickets must not be issued for any purpose other than early morning single journeys. This is important, in order to permit of an analysis of early morning single tickets issued.

15. Children's fares are based on half the adult single fare, fractions of ½d. being charged as ½d.

16. When tickets are required for fare values not covered by the range on the machine, two or more tickets will be issued in combination and torn off as one ticket. The class knob must be set at the appropriate class for the first ticket, and at "COM" for the additional ticket(s) required.

17. In the event of an ordinary single ticket being issued at the same time as an early morning single ticket to enable a passenger to travel on beyond the finishing point of the early morning single ticket, both tickets must be printed with the stage number at which the passenger boards the vehicle. The tickets will be issued in combination and torn off as one ticket, the class knob being set at "EMS" for the first ticket, and at "COM" for the additional ticket(s) required.

18. In the event of an error on the part of a conductor or a passenger, whereby a ticket is issued but is not required, the conductor must withdraw the ticket issued, see that the passenger is provided with a correct ticket and make any appropriate cash adjustment. He must hand in the withdrawn ticket with the machine at the close of duty, together with a report of the mistake and the name and address of the passenger concerned ; conductors cannot be credited with the amount involved unless this procedure is carried out.

Fare stages

19. The fare stage number on the machine must be re-set as each fare stage is reached.

At end of journey

20. Upon completion of each journey, enter in the appropriate positions in the journey column on the cash total sheet the figures appearing on the corresponding fare value counters and the total counter on the machine.

Auxiliary way-bill

21. Whenever a conductor is relieved, he must prepare and hand over to the relief an auxiliary way-bill showing the starting number on the total counter at the commencement of that journey, and the reading on the total counter at the time of handing over.

PROCEDURE ON COMPLETION OF DUTY

22. By reference to the cash total sheet : —

    (a) Enter in the appropriate "Register readings" column the readings from **each of the fourteen** fare value counters and the total counter.

    (b) Enter in the appropriate "Quantity sold" column the differences between the starting and closing numbers recorded against each fare value and "Total".

    (c) Check that the total quantity sold entered in accordance with (b) above agrees with the total obtained by adding up the entries shown in the "Quantity sold" column. Should a discrepancy arise, check all calculations.

    (d) Enter in the appropriate "£. s. d." column the cash value of the tickets sold at each fare value. Add up these amounts and enter the total in the space provided.

23. The cash total sheet must then be completed in the normal way and handed, together with the machine and container, to the Depot Inspector on duty who will check to ensure that the total counter reading on the machine agrees with that entered on the cash total sheet.

Appendix 4:
Commemorative Tickets

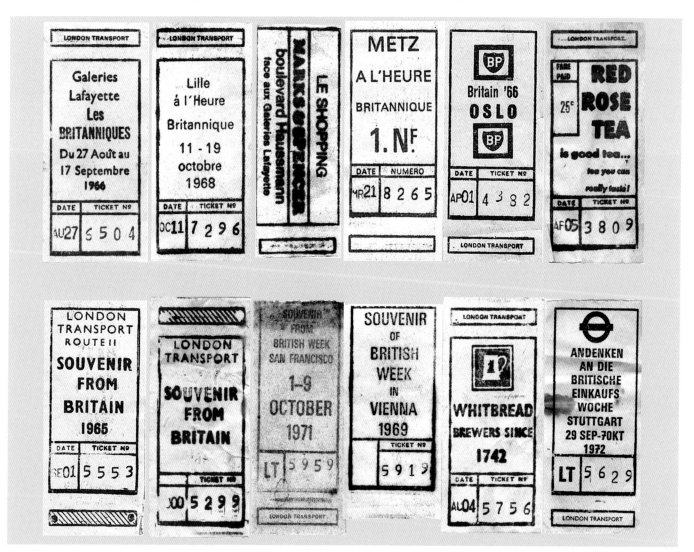

This page and next page: Commemorative tickets issued by Gibson machines in conjunction with special events and overseas tours to promote Britain and British industry. Many date from the 1960s when a balance of payments crisis meant devaluation of Sterling and the launch of the campaign 'I'm Backing Britain' in 1968.

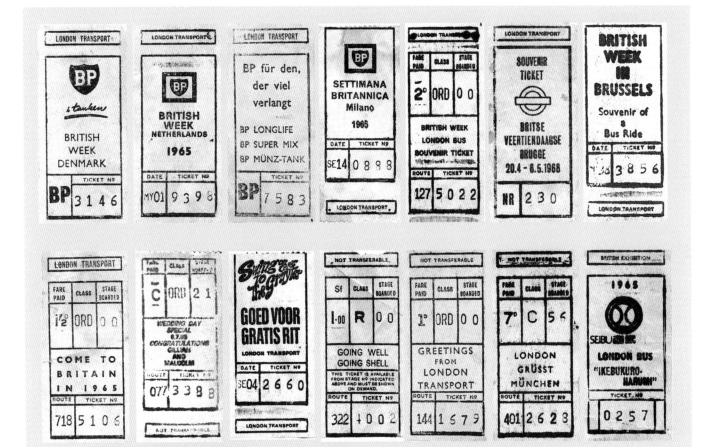

Left: The last Gibson variant to produce commemorative tickets dated from 1985 and was used for rides on the skid bus during a Chiswick open day. The print plate was made of rubber. None of the moveable type from the donor machine was utilised.

Appendix 5:
Clipper Conversion Dates by Garage/ Operating Company and Routes

Garage	Operating Co.	Routes affected	Changeover date from Gibson to Clipper machines
Tottenham	Leaside	73	Phased introduction from 02/11/1992 to 15/03/1993
Camberwell	London Central	12, 137	19/04/1993
Nine Elms	Kentish Bus	19	24/04/1993
Norwood	South London	2	27/04/1993
Chalk Farm	London Northern	139	29/04/1993
Bow	East London	8	10/05/1993
Clapton	Leaside	38	11/05/1993
Finchley	London Northern	13	14/05/1993
Willesden	Metroline	6, 98	17/05/1993
Putney	London General	14, 22	19/05/1993
Brixton	South London	137, 159	26/05/1993
Upton Park	East London	15	27/05/1993
New Cross	London Central	36	19/06/1993 [1]
Waterloo	London General	11	17/07/1993 [2]
Holloway	London Northern	10, 139	31/07/1993
Shepherds Bush	London United	9, 94	19/08/1993
Westbourne Park	Centrewest	7, 23	23/08/1993

1. Date of takeover of crew buses from Peckham garage
2. On closure of Victoria garage